SUPER
GRUB

Collins

MALCOLM GLUCK

SUPER GRUB

SILVENA ROWE

Dinner-party bliss on a budget

First published in 2004 by
Collins, an imprint of
HarperCollins *Publishers*
77-85 Fulham Palace Road
Hammersmith
London W6 8JB

The Collins website address is www.collins.co.uk

Collins is a registered trademark of HarperCollins Publishers Ltd

10	09	08	07	06	05	04
7	6	5	4	3	2	1

Editor: Susan Fleming
Design: Bob Vickers

A catalogue record for this book is available from the British Library

ISBN 0-00-717612-0

Printed in Great Britain by Clays Ltd, St Ives plc

To Rosie and Eric and everyone at Books for Cooks
for introducing me to Silvena.

M.G.

To my boys — Malcolm, Illen and Alex.

S.R.

'I look upon it that he who does not mind his belly will hardly mind anything else.'

Samuel Johnson

'It is considered no longer actually wrong, but certainly ignoble to concern oneself passionately with the quality of food and wine.'

Raymond Postgate,
The Good Food Guide, 1969

CONTENTS

CONTENTS

INTRODUCTION
by Malcolm Gluck

This book has had a long genesis (much longer than the biblical variety). It began at 9.30 in the evening on the 29th of May 1964. It was then that I first saw intriguing food being consumed alongside fascinating wine. I was in France, of course. Until then I had imagined food was fuel and wine was Moroccan, seven shillings and sixpence the bottle, and not especially subtle or mind-stretching. After my French experience, which occurred in a town called Gaillac, upon my return to England I devoted myself to food and wine, learned to cook, studied everything printed on wine and drank everything bottled on the same subject.

After becoming a wine writer for the *Guardian* some twenty-five years after this, I had an idea to extend my remit. I wrote a book with Antony Worrall Thompson called *SuperNosh* (1993). This matched his food ideas with the wines I selected. However, it was just food ideas. It wasn't fully worked-out recipes, let alone menus, and nothing was based on value for money (except my wines).

After this, a much better idea came to me called *Twenty-QuidCuisine*. This was to be a book (based on a popular newspaper column I hoped), which devoted itself to a terrific chef providing a meal for four and with me coming up with sufficient wines – all for £20. By the time the idea appealed to the *Guardian*, in 2002, prices had moved on and *TwentyQuidCuisine* could refer only to the cost of the food. The wine, under my suggested title of *TenQuidTipples*, cost extra.

Thus, 'Party Paupers' (the fresh, slightly misleading, firmly ambiguous *Guardian* name for Silvena's and my joint column published every other Wednesday in the G2 supplement) came to pass. And this subsequent book, based on those columns, under the title *SuperGrub*, was born. What neither title gives a hint of is that money underpins how Silvena picks her ingredients as much as it does how I choose the wines. Each of the dishes is costed out and the whole meal, for four, costs less than £20 to prepare (though some ingredients have their costs amortised over several menus). I stick, in my initial recommendations, to finding sufficient wine for four people for a tenner or less. But I cheat like mad at times too. The temptation is just too great.

This lengthy journey of the book in your hands is proof of Oscar Wilde's remark that nothing worth learning can be taught. No school, no book, could ever have taught me what I now know about newspaper columns and publishers. I had to learn it myself; at first hand, by experience. What is worth learning is begun by inspiration (or seduction), fuelled by necessity or unbridled enthusiasm, enhanced by practice.

To be sure, you can discover a lot about wine itself by observing how good tasters do it, and if such lessons are related to sensory exploration, then this approach has much to recommend it. But how can you learn about finding the right wine for the food except by doing it? And doing it regularly? Education in food and wine matching is largely self-education. It is personal. It is just like sex. To which, of course, wine and food are intimately related since all these activities are adventures of those same subjective senses (to which we owe unswerving allegiance as we see them as indivisible from our selves like our limbs and organs).

MARRYING WINE AND FOOD

We, Silvena and I, fervently hope, with confidence, that this book will inspire you to make all the discoveries to be made in food and wine for yourself. Each of us has her and his own journey to make, and though that sounds pretty soppy it is true; but once started, the road, with all its delicious by-ways and alleys off, never seems to fail to fascinate or, crucially, to end. I never cease to make discoveries in food and wine matching. An open mind is as important as an open mouth (more so, in fact, as a hunger for food and refreshment is merely an animal instinct whereas the hunger for new ideas and fresh experiences is more human).

Now many of us enjoy wine simply as drink, and in this respect it has taken the place of beer in many Britons' so-called 'drinking repertoires'. However, wine enhances food and adds to the pleasure of its consumption. It will render harmless many of the bacteria associated with food and which may cause stomach upsets. In other words, wine is a benign killer. It aids digestion.

However, wine and food together make a wonderful marriage and it is one of the most neglected, and least appreciated, aspects of wine criticism. Many wine critics are more concerned with the elements of the soil of the vineyard, or desperate to identify the chemicals in the wine which cause it to smell and taste the way it does, than to develop the appetite to always consider the reason why wine is so widely grown in the first place: to accompany food and to heighten the pleasure of its consumption.

It's all subjective Where wine and food as matched entities are concerned, the same applies. This book can only succeed above all else by inspiring its readers to try its food and wine matching ideas and discovering the true learning process to which this will lead. Taste is individual, not only in matters of taste but on grounds of biology, and what you may sense as sweet I may discern as acidic. The range of flavours which can confront the palate, like shades of colours the eye, and sounds of music the ear, is a subjective experience. These experiences do not exist, in fact, in the objective world; they exist because of subatomic vibrations – resulting in our brains converting them to colours, smells and sounds – and each of us will bring a unique bearing to each. And the same is even more emphatically true when taste and smell are both involved and, with food and wine matching (as will be discussed in a moment), even more complex reactions.

That said, let me make one thing clear. If you enjoy vintage port with cornflakes or Barolo with smoked salmon then no-one can tell you you're wrong. No-one has precisely the same ideas when it comes to food and wine matching. This is not just some liberal notion by the way; not starred-eyed democratic idealism; it is a proven scientific fact beyond the mere differences between individuals.

How? Because each human, as do all vertebrate animals, generates saliva. The make-up of this liquid forms a massive part of the intake of all of us, several litres a day if we're men (considerably less if we're a woman), and it is a natural part of the body's make-up. Saliva is made up of proteins, salts and an enzyme called amylase. Its purpose is to aid digestion; it actually disperses compounds such is its strength and purpose, and each person's is individual to that person. This, allied to other physiological dispositions which make us unique individuals, means we taste things purely on an individual basis (and, of course, our perceptions of food and wine can change on a daily basis also because the recipe for each day's saliva can be affected by our mood and physical state).

I discovered the truth of this some years after my apotheosis in Gaillac. In 1972, I was sitting in the corner of a French restaurant, Le Français in the Fulham Road in London, reading a book (Iris Murdoch has just brought out *The Black Prince*). While waiting for my cassoulet and sipping, or rather chewing, a glass of Cahors, a wine so thickly clotted you could grease axles with it, I devoured Miss Murdoch as eagerly as I expected I would consume my cassoulet. There now arrived an old cove and he put himself down, like some ancient battered suitcase, into the adjacent seat at the next table. He apologised for disturbing me, noted the book, and muttered he liked history too. He was then joined by a disturbingly gorgeous young woman who made even Iris's charms pale.

I tried to concentrate on my book, but how could I? The old cove ordered turbot, for himself and his companion, and Jean-Jacques Figeac (the chef) was instructed to cook it rare so that 'the bones show up pink', and to go with this he told the sommelier to bring him a bottle of 1949 Château Pape Clément.

I was thunderstruck. A red Graves, and a very old one at that, with a half-cooked turbot? Unbelievable. But do you know something? That old man and his young guest had the most marvellous time. They loved the food; they adored the wine; they laughed fit to burst at each other's bon mots. And here was me, who thought he knew his onions, with his regulation cassoulet and dutiful Cahors, and I realised I was being taught a great lesson in how to live, and how to match wine with food, and it would be a crime not to remember it.

Red with fish? The secret of that marriage, I discovered later upon investigation, was that the tinges of blood in the fish and the tannins in the wine affected a protein interchange, rather as happens, though on a more spectacular scale, with very rare roast beef and tannic claret. Tannin is, after all, an antioxidant which the grape produces, like many plants, as protection. It makes animal skins more supple. It softens rare meat. It all makes chemical sense, but above all it makes beautiful sensory sense. The rule, then, that fish can only be eaten with white wine is a load of old cobblers. I have since found that grilled salmon, on the rare side, not over-cooked, with Australian

Cabernet Sauvignon or chilled Pinot Noir is a superb combination.

In South Africa I have often been offered Pinotage with grilled local seafood delicacies, and the marriage works perfectly. Indeed, you can drink any young, fresh, fruity wine like Pinotage from the Cape or Syrah from the Languedoc, or Kekfrancos from Hungary or Blauer Zweigelt from Austria or Valpolicella Classico from Italy or Chinon or Bourgueil from the Loire or Pinot Noir from Alsace with fish. Serve the wine lightly chilled and the effects will be even better. I was lucky enough to be taken for a birthday treat to the London celebrity haunt, Nobu, an ambitious Japanese restaurant with many startling culinary ideas, and I insisted on drinking well-chilled Chinon with the signature dish of blackened cod and another dish of lobster. My host and hostess, a generous couple who had, politely, raised eyebrows when I chose the wine from the list (not least because it was one of the most affordable in an otherwise expensive vinous catalogue), were delighted when they experienced this red with their fish dishes.

Spices and wine Nowadays we eat a much wider repertoire of dishes from all over the world. We eat spicier food. The single most widely consumed dish in the UK is chicken tikka, I believe. Can any French or Spanish or Italian wine go with it? Well, a few. But much more willing to sit down with oriental food are the wines of the New World. They were made (by accident, but it is a happy accident) for these dishes. Thus the old rules, those old Victorian maxims that made etiquette dictate hock with the halibut and Bordeaux with the beef, have gone out of the window.

I eat lots of fish and drink lots of red wine. I often pair the two. Of course, smoked fish or shellfish are best with white wines. But even here there are no rules. I once drank the *Jurassic Park* actor Sam Neill's home-grown Pinot Noir with his Japanese wife's dish of green-lipped mussels, and it was terrific. I was surprised. I learned something invaluable.

It is useful to remember that the main ingredient of a dish is not, when deciding on the wine, the one that is the most important. If any of the fish dishes just mentioned had contained a lot of chillies or turmeric or coriander or ginger, then a red wine would not work at all. In these instances, an Alsatian Pinot Gris or Gewürztraminer has more to recommend it as do German Rieslings of a Spätlese level of ripeness and richness.

If you are having lamb, for instance, but neglect to consider that it is stuffed with a spicy forcemeat and comes with a saffron sauce, then you cannot find the right wine. A slab of cod, say, is to be the proffered bride to a chosen wine, but in fact the wine will have to marry with a caper sauce rather than the fish. Prawns, said a man to me once, we're having prawns, forgetting to point out that they were to be marinated in a Thai dip and barbecued. One of the best restaurants in Cornwall is Sevens in Truro, owned by *Guardian* readers Jane and David White. They invited me to dinner there, and I had a most enjoyable starter of scallops and black pudding, with a white wine made from the Gros Manseng grape from the Béarn. With the turbot and fennel to follow I drank Raats Wooded Chenin Blanc from the Cape but the sauce, which contained saffron, overpowered the wine (and there was no suggestion from the description of the dish on the menu that the fish would come with such a potent sauce). Had I known this I would have chosen a different wine, for even though the Raats is well wooded, it is delicate and a wine with more fruit is needed with saffron.

In other words, always consider the strongest ingredients in a dish, not just the biggest (and the most expensive) component of it. I was once offered a well-cooked duck dish but it was only when I tasted the curious sweet-yet-savoury sauce that accompanied it that I realised I should find a big, rich red wine to go with it, not a floral-scented white as I had initially imagined.

Good food wines German Riesling, which fits that floral description, has an important place in food and wine matching. It is whistle-clean and subtle, with a beautiful texture to the fruit. It has a touch of honey with balancing acids, and it is these two which make it so staunch a friend alongside the spicy foods of India, Thailand, China, Pakistan, Bangladesh and Japan, Indonesia and the so-called ethnic fusion cooking of the trendier eateries. At the Cinnamon Club restaurant in London, which boasts some of Europe's most adventurous Indian food, I had a spice-encrusted bream with a marvellous raw mango chutney (a Kerala dish) but the wine with it, a fairly mature Australian Sémillon, was too dry, and the right wine, like a German Auslese, would have provided the fruit which would have matched that fierce, though perhaps genteel at heart, chutney. Aussie Sémillon, one of the world's most under-appreciated white wines, is great with bream ordinarily, but not if there are certain lively spices present on the plate.

Alsatian wines are no less versatile. Wines from this incredibly dry and beautiful part of France also work with oriental food yet they also work with more European dishes. Alsatian Gewürztraminer with cheese? Absolutely. In Alsace they always pair this wine with the local Munster, which though gracious on the palate, smells like a crowded inner-city gym on a humid Saturday morning. Bries and Camemberts, and certain goats' cheeses, also work with Gewürztraminer.

Tokay-Pinot Gris is fine with well-cooked game dishes where there is a fruity sauce. Such food does not necessarily demand a red wine accompaniment. With a cherry sauce or cassis-based sauce or gravy, the apricot richness of the wine goes superbly with the meat. Try Riesling with roast chicken. Alsatian Riesling is richer than German, a touch raunchier and feistier. Roast chicken and tarragon with such a wine, especially if it's a few years old, can be a sublime match.

Let me offer a few other sublime marriage ideas. Australian Shiraz works with curries. Cava, the Spanish bubbly, loves smoked salmon. Red Rioja, not too old, not over-wooded, enjoys fishcakes. South African Pinotage thrills to find itself with pasta with pesto sauce and bacon bits. Manzanilla sherry seems made for stir-fried prawns. Rumanian Pinot Noir and roast chicken with mushrooms are perfect together. Parmesan risotto and Chianti get on together as cosily as Sally Tripe and Sid Onions. Australian Sémillon with chicken Kiev is a remarkable union. Thai fish dishes with New Zealand Sauvignon Blancs are difficult to beat. Montilla, from Spain, turns fish and chips into something special.

And, to finish any meal or introduction, ice-cream (not to mention Greek yoghurt and honey) with Moscatel de Valencia is a dream team (yet equally interesting is to use a sweet sherry which you can also pour over the ice-cream). Times have changed since Raymond Postgate caught the mood of the times in his introduction to the 1969 *Good Food Guide* (as quoted in the frontispiece of this book). To concern oneself with how a particular dish works with a particular wine is now, in this day and age, not only civilised, but proof you care about how you live. Could it, indeed, be one of the secrets of a long and happy life?

IMPORTANT THOUGHTS ON WINE VINTAGES, PRICES, RETAILERS AND RATINGS

Vintages

Many of the wines which appear with each menu carry vintage dates, as first published in the newspaper. Most of these wines, the great majority indeed, are now in a newer vintage and it cannot be assumed that the wine is exactly the same or that it works with the same dish in precisely the same way as the older wine. Why have we retained these vintages? Because in spite of what I have just said, it is also true that most of these wines are of a style which may not vary hugely from vintage to vintage and so it is useful to know what these wines were because the infomation is valuable in making another choice. However, what is also true is that these vintage variations would in some cases eliminate a wine from candidature with a particular dish. It is rare that a wine would be so different, so vividly different from one vintage to the next, that it could not be enjoyed with a particular dish, but it may not be the perfect choice. To widen the choice of wines available, I have also suggested other bottles, some in generic terms on stylistic grounds, to go with each menu and these are also, of course, subject to vintage variations, but again I am confident that these variations would not make one wine of one vintage wholly inappropriate compared with a wine of an earlier or later vintage. It was, in truth, impossible to offer totally specific wines with each and every dish as the book would then be out of date within months of writing (since it has to be prepared a few months before its October publication date).

Prices

These are correct at time of writing, but may change due to alterations in alcohol duty and price hikes by retailers. But no price should differ so wildly from the one given as to make it dramatic. In some instances I have given an approximate as a guide where non-specific bottles are mentioned.

Retailers

Most of the wines said to be at a particular retailer will still be there, albeit in different vintages in many instances. For the wines which meet my initial criterion of coming in at under a tenner for four people (often that means two or three bottles), it is obvious that the supermarkets and high street wine chains are the places to look. As I expand the choices of bottles, and extend the retail remit to any wine merchant whose wine takes my fancy, any price can apply and any address in the country (where a retailer may have just one shop although offering a mail-order facility). A list of contact details of all retailers mentioned is on page 203.

Rating

It is worth repeating: value for money is my single unwavering focus. I drink with my readers' pockets in my mouth. I do not see the necessity of paying a lot for a bottle of wine to go with food, especially when I am working under the disciplines of what I call *TenQuidTipples* (ie enough wine for four people for dinner for under a tenner all in). A few times in this book, I adjust the rating to take account of the peculiar affinity of the wine with the dish, and its rating applies only in these circumstances.

I do taste expensive wines regularly. I do not, regularly, find them worth the money. That said, there are some pricey bottles in these pages because they suit the foods. A wine of magnificent complexity, thrilling fruit, superb aroma, great depth and finesse is worth drinking – if it will enhance the food. Such a wine challenges the intellect as much as the palate and its value lies, like a great theatrical performance or outstanding novel, in its unforgettableness. I will rate it highly. Even though it costs a lot, the lot it costs is justified, and if it makes the dining experience that much more memorable, you may consider the expense worth it.

20 points Is outstanding and faultless in all departments: smell, taste and finish in the throat. Worth the price, even if you have to take out a second mortgage. Life rarely throws up perfection. Indeed, some aesthetes regard true beauty as always revealing a small flaw. I do not. There is no flaw in a 20-point wine. It has perfect balance, finesse, flavour and finish – dull terms to describe the sum of an unforgettable experience. A perfect wine is also perfectly affordable. That is not to say (necessarily) £2.99 or even £4.99, but a sum related to common sense. Even if such a wine costs £100 it is still worth 20 points and the possible pain of acquisition. I exclude from this auction-antiques which cost thousands of pounds, for these are the perverted passions of wine collectors and the prices paid rarely bear any relation to the quality of the liquid in the bottles. No wine is truly worth thousands of pounds and no roundly civilised individual would pay it.

19 points A superb wine. Almost perfect and well worth the expense (if it is an expensive bottle). What's a point between friends? Or between one wine and another? 19 points represents a superb wine of towering individuality and impact. Almost perfect and well worth the expense (even if it is an expensive bottle), such a wine will flood the senses with myriad smells, tastes and flavours and provide a tantalising glimpse, whilst it lasts, of the sheer textured genius of great wine. Such a wine is individual, rich, subtle yet potent, and overwhelmingly delicious. It can start, and finish, a conversation – with or without food.

18 points An excellent wine but lacking that ineffable sublimity of richness and complexity to achieve the very highest rating. Such a wine offers superb drinking and thundering good value and it must exhibit a remarkably well-textured richness. True, I do emphasise texture above other aspects of complexity (like all those fruits some tasters are determined to find in a wine) and here the texture is so well married to the acids and sugars that it is all of a piece. Such a wine is remarkable, immensely drinkable, complex and compelling.

17 points An exciting, well-made wine at an affordable price which offers real glimpses of multi-layered richness. It will demonstrate individuality and incisiveness and it will offer a seductive mouthfeel and sense of luxury. It may be a more immediate wine than those rating higher, but it will still linger in the memory the day after it is drunk – for it will have given a delightful and impressive performance.

16 points This is a very good wine indeed. Good enough for any dinner party and any level of drinker (with the possible exception of those most toffee-nosed of snobs for whom pleasure usually comes associated with a large price tag). Not necessarily an expensive wine is implied here, but it will be a terrifically drinkable, satisfying and multi-dimensional bottle. It will be properly balanced and often be excellent with particular kinds of dishes (which it enhances).

15 points For the money, a good mouthful with real style. Good flavour and fruit without costing a packet. A 15-point rating when applied to a food wine is extremely valuable; for a wine which might not impress in an hierarchical wine-tasting alongside other bottles can be excellent with food. Many such wines are also bottles on promotional offer, reduced in price for a certain period. A feature of the UK wine scene is the constant appearance of such wines and they are of great value to the entertaining, generous host and hostess who pay heed to a sensible budget.

14 points The top end of everyday drinking wine. Well made and to be seriously recommended at the price. Such rating, as I say with the 15 pointers, when applied to a food wine is important; for a wine which might not impact greatly when tasted alongside other bottles can be excellent with food. In instances where there is a large party with a lot of thirsts, and the food is robust and/or spicy, then many a 14-pointer must not be denied its place at table just because it is so inexpensive.

13 points and below No wine which scores less than 14 points appears in this book, though superplonk.com, my website, lists hundreds (if not thousands) of such bottles. These wines have not aroused my enthusiasm, either because they are so expensive as to be absurd or simply lacking in an essential element. It is redundant for me to add anything further.

NOTE Where a wine does not carry a rating, it is to be assumed that it is worth a minimum of 16 points with the dish.

INTRODUCTION
by Silvena Rowe

I always remember a comment made by the Roux brothers when they referred to their mother who brought them up in the firm belief that good food should not be expensive. She was absolutely right, but many chefs would still have us believe that good food is and has to be expensive. As a chef, I have always cooked the best food for the best possible price, and to achieve this I have always stayed faithful to the seasons, for it is in season that produce is not only at its best, but also at its cheapest.

In the last ten years, I have cooked for many of the rich and famous and I can honestly say that everyone, regardless of their financial standing, wants value for money when it comes down to food. So we decided to put it all into practice and to set a challenge – inspirational and exciting food for four people but within a budget of £20 – and it works. The *Guardian* columns, which have inspired this book, have been hugely successful and you have all asked for the recipes, time and time again.

So here is the book, with its unpredictable and surprisingly delicious food at a cost-effective price. I hope that everyone will continue to enjoy the challenge that the recipes in the book present to the imagination and that are demanded by the budgetary challenge!

LIST OF RECIPES

COLD STARTERS

HOT STARTERS

SOUPS

FISH MAIN COURSES

MEAT MAIN COURSES

POULTRY MAIN COURSES

VEGETABLE, RICE AND GRAIN MAIN COURSES

DESSERTS

DESSERT CAKES AND BISCUITS

All eggs are large and free-range.

All recipes are for four unless otherwise specified.

AUTUMN

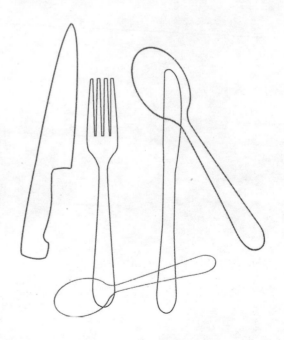

GARDEN SALAD with ROASTED GARLIC VINAIGRETTE and SOY-ROASTED COBNUTS

The cobnut tree is a common tree in woods and hedgerows throughout Britain. The season is very short so you should gather some whenever you venture for a park or country walk in early autumn. But if you are not the outdoor type, then visit your local farmers' market where you can buy those wonderful, crunchy, sweet nuts. They are particularly delicious when just roasted with some soy sauce.

handful of shelled cobnuts
soy sauce
Maldon salt
300g mixed salad leaves, washed and dried

Vinaigrette
1 garlic bulb, unpeeled
olive oil
60ml extra virgin olive oil
juice of 1 lemon
salt and pepper

Preheat the oven to 180°C/350°F/Gas 4.

For the vinaigrette, place the garlic on a suitably sized piece of foil and drizzle with some olive oil. Wrap it and place in the oven to roast for 20 minutes. Let it cool. The garlic is now very creamy and soft within its skin. All you have to do is squeeze the paste out as though you were squeezing toothpaste out of a tube.

To make the vinaigrette, place the soft garlic paste in a small bowl together with the extra virgin olive oil and the lemon juice. Mix well and season.

To prepare the cobnuts, crush them gently and place on a baking tray, drizzle with some soy sauce and sprinkle generously with Maldon salt. Bake for about 5–7 minutes, until slightly roasted. Let them cool.

Finally to make the salad, toss the leaves with the vinaigrette and sprinkle generously with the soy-roasted cobnuts.

COST £2.80

SPICED NEW SEASON FILLET of VENISON

Venison is a wonderful, tender and flavourful meat. I have chosen to feature a recipe with it as the new venison season has just begun in early autumn. One of the best ways of preparing venison is to marinate it in advance, and the method below requires marinating overnight.

4 venison fillets, about 150g each
2 tbsp hazelnut oil

Marinade
1 x 2cm piece galangal, peeled and chopped
2 lemongrass stalks, white part only, finely chopped
finely grated rind and segments of 1 lime
40g caster sugar
1 small red chilli, finely chopped
handful of chopped cobnuts
80g tomato paste
coriander roots, washed well and chopped (from 1 bunch
    coriander)
Thai fish sauce, to taste

For the marinade, combine the galangal, lemongrass, lime rind and segments, sugar, chilli and cobnuts in a food processor and work into a fine paste. Add the tomato paste, coriander roots and fish sauce to taste, and blend again. Rub the marinade well on to the venison fillets, cover with clingfilm, and place in the refrigerator overnight.

When ready to cook, heat the oil in a heavy skillet until very hot, and smoking. Pan-fry the venison fillets for about 3–5 minutes on each side, depending on how well cooked you like them. I like venison served very pink, so I cook mine for about 3 minutes on each side. Serve with plain boiled Thai rice.

Cost £14.10

DAMSON FOOL served with TOASTED COBNUTS

The French have mirabelles and we have damsons....Damsons, one of the glories of early autumn, are quintessentially English. They tend to be rather sour and require quite a bit of sugar, unless you like your plum puds very tart! Pick-your-own is in full swing just now, so find where you can do this locally. Failing that, farmers' markets are ideal. Damsons are also perfect for jams and pickles.

400g damsons, washed and pitted
80g caster sugar, or more if you like your fool sweeter
250ml double cream
2 tbsp mascarpone cheese
finely grated zest of 1 orange
handful of shelled cobnuts, lightly toasted

Place the damsons and the sugar in a pan, add 2 tbsp water, and stir over a very low heat until the sugar has dissolved. Simmer for another 10 minutes or until the damsons are soft and have become gooey. Rub the mixture through a sieve and taste to see if more sugar is required.

Whip the double cream to soft peaks, add the mascarpone and orange zest, and fold the damson mixture in gently. Place in glasses and chill for about 3 hours. Serve with the toasted cobnuts sprinkled on top.

COST £3.10

THE WINE SELECTION

Silvena does not know this but I am, and have been for several decades, a cobnutter. I get through two bags of the little brown orbs a fortnight and in season, I have been known to trek to Richmond Park where there is a copse of cobnut trees, and plunder them of everything I can carry. Sad though it may be to contemplate so seemingly innocent, naïve, so basic an obsession, an evening of heady excitement for me is to be sat before an absorbing book with a hearty bottle of red wine and huge bowl of the nuts.

I daresay this week's menu might tempt me to abandon these pursuits and come to table but the hearty red will have to come with me. Such a red will have to combat some wily spicing in the salad with its roasted garlic vinaigrette and it will have a further hurdle, a veritable Beecher's Brook indeed, with the venison's spice rub. Money no object I'd go for a robust, sweetly berried St Chinian from a warm and herby corner of the Midi called **Laurent Miquel 2001** which, rating **17.5 points**, costs £11.99 at **www.sainsburys.co.uk/wine**. But this boisterously rich red wine blows my budget and so, to cope with both starters and main course, we must be less extravagant and so I am going to suggest a neighbour of the St Chinian. This is **Asda's** own-label non-vintage **Corbières** at a ridiculous £2.97 a bottle. Rating **16 points**, it flaunts delicious strawberry and blackberry fruit with biscuity tannins and shows real texture and class.

I reckon three bottles of this red will see us nicely through the meal leaving us with £1.09 for a wine to accompany that damson fool. Clearly an impossible task. Tsk tsk. But cannot this book break any rule (even its own)? Can it not venture where other wine critics fear to tread? That said, we shall splash out on **Aldi's** sumptuous **St Amandus Beerenauslese 2001 (16 points, £2.99)** from Germany in the 50cl bottle. This unguent dessert wine offers the flavours of Greek honey and sweet white peach and is, frankly, sheer bottled hedonism.

Menu 2   ROASTED BEETROOT with LEMON THYME and LEMON OIL
           SMOKED HADDOCK with BEETROOT and SWEET POTATOES
                         BASIL ICE-CREAM with BASIL JUS

ROASTED GOLDEN BEETROOT with LEMON THYME and LEMON OIL

Burpees Golden, the famous orange beetroot, is just in season. It is both sweet and savoury, so here is a whole menu inspired by it. In season also is the new lemon thyme, a great partner to orange beetroot. For the best lemon oil on the market, head for The Fresh Olive Company (mail order 020 8453 1918).

8 medium-sized Burpees Golden beetroots
6 tbsp finely chopped lemon thyme leaves
6 tbsp lemon oil
handful of garlic cloves, unpeeled
chunky sea salt

Preheat the oven to 220°C/425°F/Gas 7.

Wash the beets well, but do not peel. Slice them into quarters and mix together with the chopped lemon thyme, lemon oil, garlic cloves and salt to taste. Coat all the beet pieces well with the mixture. Roast in the preheated oven for 12 minutes, then reduce the heat to 180°C/350°F/Gas 4 and roast for another 25 minutes. The colour of the cooked beets should be slightly brown.

Serve immediately while hot, accompanied by a salad of crunchy beet leaves simply tossed in your favourite vinaigrette.

COST £ 4.50

PAN-FRIED SMOKED HADDOCK with BEETROOT PURÉE and SAUTÉED SWEET POTATOES

Don't buy the bright yellow coloured haddock, it contains dye. Instead ask your fishmonger to get you the lightly lemon coloured smoked haddock which has been prepared more naturally. All these wonderful ingredients have the warm colours of an Indian summer.

4 fillets smoked haddock, about 150g each
100ml milk
handful of plain flour
olive oil
2 large orange-fleshed sweet potatoes, peeled and
    sliced into discs 1cm thick

Beet purée
2 shallots, finely chopped
1 tbsp lemon thyme leaves
2 rashers smoked bacon
4 large Burpees Golden beetroots, washed, peeled and
    chopped into small pieces
50ml double cream
salt and pepper

First of all remove the skin of the haddock. This is not difficult but you do need confidence, so if uncertain then ask your fishmonger to do it for you. Place the fish pieces in a flat dish and pour over the milk. Let stand for a couple of hours.

Meanwhile prepare the beet purée. Sweat the shallot and thyme in 1 tbsp olive oil, then add the bacon and continue cooking. Add the beet pieces and cook until they are soft, about 20 minutes. Finally add the cream and simmer for few more minutes. Remove the bacon. Season to taste, liquidise and pass through a chinois or other sieve. Keep warm.

Now take the haddock out of the milk and dry well with kitchen paper. Coat the fish with plain flour. Heat about 2 tbsp olive oil in a heavy frying pan and, when hot enough, pan-fry the haddock for about 3 minutes each side.

To prepare the sweet potatoes, boil them for about 3 minutes until only semi-soft. Drain them well and sauté in about 2 tbsp hot olive oil until browned.

To serve, spoon some beet purée on to the middle of each serving plate and place a fillet of pan-fried smoked haddock on the top. Accompany on the side with sautéed sweet potatoes.

COST £10.80

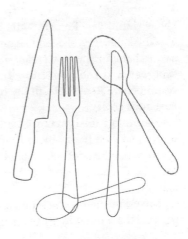

BASIL ICE-CREAM with BEET JUS

A basil-flavoured, satiny ice-cream with a sophisticated fragrance, that is beautifully complemented not only by the flavour, but by the colour too, of the silky and sleek beet jus. To obtain beetroot juice, simply peel and chop about two beetroot, and put the pieces into a juicer. They are very juicy when raw.

Ice-cream
480ml double cream
large bunch of fresh basil, leaves only
2 tbsp finely grated orange zest
4 egg yolks
90g caster sugar

Beet jus
50ml white wine vinegar
80ml beetroot juice (see above)
juice and finely grated zest of ½ orange
100g caster sugar

For the ice-cream, bring the cream to the boil with half of the basil and all the orange zest. Remove from the heat, and leave to infuse for about 35 minutes. Return to the heat again to boil briefly.

Whisk the egg yolks and sugar together until thick and creamy, and slowly pour in the hot cream. Mix well, then pour it back into the saucepan and cook on a low heat for a further 3 minutes, stirring continuously. Remove from the heat. Keep stirring constantly until the custard is cool.

Pour into a food processor, adding the rest of the basil, and purée. Strain and then freeze in an ice-cream machine.

To make the beet jus, mix all the ingredients in a small pan and bring to the boil. Lower the heat and simmer for 15 minutes. Strain and reduce to a syrup.

Serve a quenelle or scoop of basil ice-cream per person, and drizzle the beet jus around it.

COST £4.60

THE WINE SELECTION

Doubtless Mrs Beeton would have approved. Or perhaps not. Silvena's way with beets is far from conventional (let alone Victorian) and she has, as is her style, taken little regard of the wine waiter (who can, as per normal, go to hell). Beetroot? All three dishes?

Roasted golden beetroot with lemon thyme and lemon oil sounds innocent enough, but the wine (which has to be white) to accompany it must have paradoxical virtues: crispness with an echo of floral spiciness. Hence I have chosen **Morrison's** non-vintage **Anjou Blanc** (**16 points**, £2.99) from the Loire which suffers from delicious double-mindedness and thus we will find it unruffled by the curious earthy yet citrussy elements in the dish. The wine offers charming under-ripe melon and citrus and I do declare that the chef will be able, as she chops and pan-fries, to slurp back the odd glass as refreshment.

For the second helping of beet, with the smoked haddock and sautéed sweet potatoes, the challenge is more definitely to find a light yet characterful red which can readily accommodate itself to being chilled. I reckon two bottles ought to do us and my hand unerringly alights on **Asda's** non-vintage **Minervois** (**15.5 points**, £2.77). This is a deft blend of 40% Grenache, 30% Syrah, 20% Carignan and 10% Mouverde which motors smoothly with an echo of coriander spiciness and offers surprisingly classy berries. With that tricky dish it is getting into bed with I think it will acquit itself handsomely.

What have we blown so far? I make it £8.53 and so we've blown it. But surely we can run to a bottle of **Moscatel de Valencia** with the basil ice-cream with its juice of the beet (or as Silvena has it, in an appalling lapse, to my mind, into trendy chef-speak, 'jus'). This honied beauty, rating **16 points**, costs £3.99 or less at all leading supermarkets (and you'll have some left over for another menu – it keeps well in the fridge). Or we can visit the **Co-op** where there is the tongue-twister called **Ilbesheimer Herrlich Beerenauslese 2001** (**16 points**, £4.49 the half bottle). Its eloquence on the tongue is aided by gorgeous spicy apricot fruit with honey, nuts and pineapple and a disposition of extreme tolerance with chilled or even icy desserts.

SICILIAN SALAD of FENNEL and ORANGES

Fennel is lovely sautéed, baked or braised as well as used raw in salads. It goes well with citrussy flavours such as orange. Apart from farmers' markets, where you are guaranteed the freshest fennel, you can get it in supermarkets. Look for fennel that has a tight head, crisp stalks and no brown spots on the white ribs.

  2 large oranges
  1 large fennel bulb
  2 tbsp olive oil
  1 tbsp lemon juice
  salt and pepper
  200g fresh wild rocket leaves
  40g pine nuts, toasted
  4 anchovies

Peel the oranges with a very sharp knife and slice into rounds. Place in a bowl.

Prepare the fennel, by trimming it first on the base and cutting away the leaves, then slice very thinly.

Add the fennel to the oranges, and add the olive oil, lemon juice and seasonings. Mix well and toss with the rocket leaves.

Sprinkle with the pine nuts, decorate with the anchovies, and serve.

COST £3.20

ROLLED CHICKEN SCHNITZEL with MUSTARD and SOURED CREAM SAUCE

This is a Bulgarian recipe, but it is also common in other parts of Eastern Europe, such as Croatia, Slovakia and Hungary. It can be prepared with veal or pork. It is usually offered on very special occasions and is considered a great delicacy.

4 large chicken breasts, each about 180g, skin removed
salt and pepper
40ml olive oil
100g chicken livers, trimmed and chopped
1 garlic clove, crushed
100g wild mushrooms, cleaned and chopped
2 tbsp plain flour

Sauce
1 shallot, finely chopped
10g streaky bacon, finely chopped
2 tbsp olive oil
1 tsp Dijon mustard
100ml white wine
100ml soured cream

Place the chicken breasts between two sheets of clingfilm and beat with a rolling pin to make them thinner. Season well.

In a frying pan heat a little of the oil and cook the chicken livers and garlic for 3 minutes, then add the wild mushrooms and stir for another couple of minutes. Leave to cool.

Divide the mushroom mixture evenly between the chicken fillets and roll them neatly into parcels. Secure with wooden cocktail sticks or use string to tie them. Roll them in the plain flour to coat well.

In a heavy sauté pan heat the rest of the oil and gently fry the rolled schnitzels, turning over continuously until they are evenly brown on all sides and cooked. This will take about 8–10 minutes.

Meanwhile make the sauce. Fry the shallot and bacon in the olive oil until softened, and then add the mustard and white wine. Simmer to reduce by half then add the soured cream. Season with salt and pepper and keep warm until ready to use.

Serve the rolled schnitzel with the sauce poured over.

COST £12.80

GREENGAGES with GRAND MARNIER ZABAGLIONE

Greengages are what the French call 'reine-claude', named after the wife of François I. Smallish and green, they are to be found at your nearest farmers' market, and occasionally in greengrocers' shops. They are the most aromatic and sweet of the plums. This simple recipe for stewed greengages is served with an elegant and light Grand Marnier zabaglione.

600g ripe greengages
4 tbsp caster sugar
2 tbsp orange juice
finely grated zest of 1 orange

Zabaglione
4 egg yolks
40g caster sugar
20ml white wine
20ml Grand Marnier

Halve and stone the greengages and place them, the sugar and orange juice in a saucepan. Cook very gently until the greengages are soft, about 5 minutes. Add the orange zest.

Meanwhile prepare the zabaglione. Beat the egg yolks and sugar together in a bowl until thick and creamy. Add the wine and Grand Marnier and sit over a bowl of simmering water. Whisk continually with an electric whisk until light, thick and frothy. This will take at least 10 minutes.

Serve the greengages and some of their juices with a dollop of zabaglione.

COST £3.90

THE WINE SELECTION

This cunningly contrived menu is full of more twists and turns than a Leonardo Sciascia thriller. It starts in Sicily (where Sciascia set his brilliant novels and stories), moves to central Europe, then drops us down somewhere between the south of France and Italy. In fact, it is Sciascia as rewritten by Ian Fleming, for it has a restless international plot and though Silvena may effortlessly play the heroine I struggle to portray the hero. What in heaven's name can comfortably snuggle up to a salad of fennel and oranges (not to mention anchovies)? This is where the prudent wine matcher steals away into the night and seeks less strenuous employment as a gold-miner or submarine dentist.

But I must persist. But where? Where is there a wine to go with that barmy salad? Ah...I have it. We require a decently aged **Moselle Auslese** from one of the Von Kesselstatt vineyards. Yes indeed! The sweetness of the wine, perfectly balanced by the acidity and minerality of the liquid, is essential; it will not blanch when faced with anchovies or oranges. Another candidate for the salad is an **Alsatian Tokay-Pinot Gris**. This has the advantage that it will also go with the chicken schnitzels with its very strong, distinctive sauce, those very gamey livers, and the wild mushrooms. It is a potent combination, this dish, and I do think it can take a strong, perfumed white wine from Alsace most definitely. Examples abound at **Oddbins** and **Majestic** and bottles crop up at the major supermarkets (though none are very mature). Two German wines which will go with the first two courses were both at **Sainsbury's** in 2002: **Bert Simon Serrig Wurtzberg Riesling Kabinett, Mosel-Saar-Ruwer 1997 (16.5 points, £6.03)** and **Querbach Oestricher Lenchen Riesling Spätlese Halbtrocken, Rheingau 1993 (16.5 points, £7.49)**. Mature, you see. It's worth paying extra for that maturity. The Bert Simon wine was superb with a hint of spicy grapefruit, fine and crisp with

petrol edging developing with the honey (suppressed under dry
peach) and there was a terrific ruffled texture. The Oestricher makes
one gasp. Ten-year-old Riesling? At this price? What an unbelievable
bargain this wine was: classy and textured with very dry citrus and
under-ripe gooseberry, a hint of aniseed and it developed gloriously
lingeringly in the throat. The past is no guarantee of the future,
philosophy teaches us, but these wines give you an excellent idea of
the kind of wine to go with this chicken dish.

Now with the greengages with their wicked Grand Marnier
zabaglione accompaniment, we require **D'Arenberg Noble Riesling
McLaren Vale 1999 (17 points, £10.99** the half bottle) from Australia.
It is strikingly original and reminds me of vinified tarte tatin. With
this dessert that wine may well make you feel you have died and
gone to heaven. You need to be alive, though, to go to **Oddbins** to
acquire it. (And if you throw at me the complaint that I have flouted
my own budgetary restrictions here, I respond, then what about the
chef? How much does Grand Marnier cost a bottle, eh?)

Menu 4 SCALLOP with BEETROOT and HORSERADISH PURÉE
LAMB and QUINCE STUFFED CABBAGE LEAVES
BAKED QUINCES in QUINCE and CINNAMON SYRUP

SEARED SCALLOP served on BEETROOT and HORSERADISH PURÉE

For this starter it is worth making an effort to get king scallops or large diver-caught scallops. You must order them specially. They are rather substantial and meaty, the best-quality scallops you can get.

4 king scallops, removed from their shell
olive oil
handful of frisée salad leaves

Beetroot and horseradish purée
4 medium beetroots, washed
4 small cauliflower florets
2 shallots, finely sliced
2 tbsp melted butter
100ml double cream
2 tsp horseradish cream
salt and pepper

Place the beetroots in a pan of boiling water and cook until soft, about 20 minutes, but more if you are using larger beets. Cool and peel off the skins. Place the beetroot in a food processor and purée. Now place the cauliflower in another saucepan of boiling water and cook until soft. Drain and purée in the food processor. (You don't need to bother cleaning out the processor goblet.)

In a very heavy pan, sweat the shallots in the butter, then add the beetroot and cauliflower, and cook slowly on a medium heat until all is thickened. Add the cream and simmer for 5 minutes. Finally add the horseradish cream and purée again in the liquidiser. Season and keep warm.

In a very heavy frying pan or cast-iron grill pan, heat a drop of oil until smoking hot and sear the scallops until browned, about 2 minutes each side.

To serve, spoon a small dollop of the beetroot purée on each serving plate, and top with a king scallop and a few salad leaves.

COST £8.20

LAMB and QUINCE STUFFED CABBAGE LEAVES

It is said that the Eskimos have numerous words for snow. And so do the people of Eastern Europe for stuffed cabbage, where stuffing cabbage leaves is almost a pastime, and it makes the most delicious and rustic meal. Cabbage is used fresh or pickled. I have slightly amended a traditional recipe by adding quince, that wonderful yellow and bumpy, pear-shaped fruit. Quinces are quintessentially English and yet there is not much mention of them in cookery books. Quinces have a wonderful perfume, and I remember as a child my Mum always keeping a fruit bowl with quinces in the kitchen, freshening the air with their delicate scent. Quinces are in season now. Adding them to savoury dishes creates delicious sweet and sour flavours.

> 1 Savoy cabbage
> 1 large quince
> 50ml lemon juice
> 1 tbsp liquid honey
> 25ml water
> *Filling*
> 350g minced lamb
> small bunch of parsley, finely chopped
> 100g long-grain rice
> 1 small onion, finely chopped
> salt and pepper

Preheat the oven to 160°C/325°F/Gas 3.

First of all prepare the cabbage by cutting out its core with a sharp knife. Place it in a large saucepan filled with hot water and simmer until the leaves are soft, about 12 minutes. Drain and carefully remove the leaves.

For the filling, mix together the lamb, parsley, rice and onion and season well.

Spread each cabbage leaf on your working surface and place a spoonful of the meat mixture in the middle. Fold over the top and roll up, tucking in both sides like a small parcel. Use wooden toothpicks to secure during cooking. Place the stuffed cabbage leaves in a single layer, seam down, in a wide but deep tray.

Peel, core and cut the quince into slices 1cm thick. Place on top of the cabbage parcels. Add the lemon juice, honey and water, and cover the tray well with foil. Place in the preheated oven and cook for about $1-1^1/2$ hours. Serve immediately.

COST £5.30

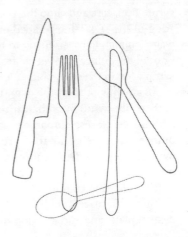

BAKED QUINCES in QUINCE and CINNAMON SYRUP

As quinces are cooked with sugar, they change colour and texture. They transform from pale yellow and woody-fleshed into brownish-red in colour and rich in flavour. In this recipe quinces are cooked in quince syrup for an even more intense flavour.

> 6 quinces
> juice of 2 lemons
> 200g caster sugar
> 1 vanilla pod, split lengthways
> 300ml water
> 4 cloves
> 1 small cinnamon stick
>
> *To serve*
> 1 small tub mascarpone cheese

Peel four of the quinces and cut them into quarters. Remove and discard the cores and place the quince flesh in a large heavy ovenproof pan with a lid, arranged in a single layer. Pour over the lemon juice to prevent discoloration.

Meanwhile, use the remaining two quinces to make the quince syrup. Peel, core and chop them coarsely. Place them in a large pan with 100g of the sugar, the scraped-out vanilla seeds and the pod. Add the water, enough to cover. Bring to the boil and simmer for about an hour or until the quinces are very soft and dark red, and the liquid has turned syrupy. Strain the syrup and discard the quince pulp and vanilla pod.

Meanwhile preheat the oven to 120°C/250°F/Gas 1/2.

Pour the syrup over the quince quarters that you prepared earlier, adding the cloves, cinnamon and remaining sugar. Make sure the quinces are covered by the syrup and place a piece of baking paper over to keep the fruit submerged. Put the lid on and cook in the preheated oven for an hour or more until the quinces are soft to the touch and red in colour.

To serve, place four quince quarters with some syrup on each dessert plate, and add a dollop of mascarpone cheese.

Cost £5.40

THE WINE SELECTION

An acquaintance examined me quizzically from head to toe recently and remarked, 'How do you stay so slim on all that food that chef of yours keeps shoving down you?' I was forced to admit that Silvena did not try out all her culinary ideas on me for she has a husband – a very large husband – and several tall hungry children for that. Most of the time, I said, all I get is an e-mail. Not much protein or carbohydrate there, I said.

And so, dear reader, do not imagine that I have scoffed scallops with beetroot and horseradish purée. I am forced to use my imagination, to sift the ingredients, to make an educated guess as to the perfect wine. In a perfect world, I'd really serve some old German Spätlese Riesling or an Alsatian Tokay-Pinot Gris with the dish but how I can I afford it? I must opt instead for **Tesco's Simply Riesling 2002** (**14.5 points**, £2.99) with its glorious screwcap. It is a German wine and has the necessary richness yet citrussiness to handle the tricky ingredients. Another excellent bet is **Aldi's Domaine Bouscau, Vin de Pays des Côtes de Gascogne 2001** (**15.5 points**, £2.99) with its delicious pineapple, pear and citrus fruit.

With the lamb-stuffed cabbage leaves we need to move on to a red wine and again we venture into **Aldi** for the own-label non-vintage **Chilean Cabernet Sauvignon** (**16 points**, £2.99). It has chocolate-undertoned berries with a touch of grilled nut and racy tannins. Two bottles should see the four of you nicely through to the pud and those baked quinces with cinnamon syrup.

With £8.97 spent we do not, as per usual, have a lot left to splash out on a dessert wine but what the hell. I unreservedly recommend **Aldi's Fletchers Cream Sherry** (**16 points**, £3.29). Its honied fruit shows toffee and crème brûlée and will help the quinces down beautifully. Alternatively, at **Safeway** there is **Concha Late Harvest Sauvignon 2000** (which has 5% Riesling as a matter of record and honied fact). This Chilean shows honey and sweet pear fruit and though rating **16 points** now, at £4.99 the half bottle, will rate **18.5 points** if cellared for eight to ten years.

PUMPKIN and ALMOND SOUP with POMEGRANATE

Pumpkins and pomegranates are two of the most exciting autumn foods. I am a well-known carnivore, but here is a temporary slip into vegetarianism. Pumpkins and pomegranates have amazing colour, texture and structure, which together create dramatic culinary effects. (They are good in soups and in risottos, as pumpkin gnocchi, made into frittata, gratins or as pumpkin tempura.) Don't go for the common Hallowe'en variety as it has little flavour and a very watery consistency. Try and get a smaller pumpkin, such as Small Sugar or Hundredweight (traditional lantern pumpkin). These are sweeter in taste, less starchy and have a denser consistency. When you are buying pomegranates, get the deep red ones.

    1 whole pumpkin, about 2kg
    olive oil
    2 large sprigs rosemary
    2 shallots, chopped
    about 1.5 litres vegetable stock (see page 197), hot
    100g ground almonds
    20g freshly grated coconut
    salt and pepper
    seeds of 1 pomegranate

Preheat the oven to 220°C/425°F/Gas 7.

Seed the pumpkin and cut into chunky cubes. Coat with olive oil, add the rosemary sprigs and shallots, and roast for at least an hour, until cooked. When cool, remove the rosemary and the pumpkin skin, and purée the pumpkin flesh and shallot.

Measure about 300ml of the hot stock and slowly pour over the ground almonds in a small saucepan, stirring all the time. Place on a medium heat and simmer gently for about 5 minutes. It should have a custard-like consistency. Add the grated coconut.

Place the puréed pumpkin in a large saucepan, add the rest of the hot stock, and season to taste. Heat through.

To serve, ladle the pumpkin soup into deep soup plates, and add some almond and coconut cream, gently swirling it over the thick soup, so that it sits on top. Sprinkle with the pomegranate seeds.

COST £4.20

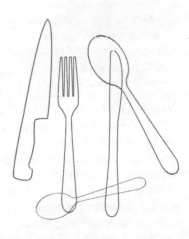

STUFFED COURGETTES with POMEGRANATE, PINE NUTS and PURPLE THAI RICE

Did you know that courgettes are actually fruits and not vegetables? They are a variety of summer squash, usually eaten when young and immature, before the seeds are capable of reproducing. Their flesh is firm and watery, the skin shiny and tender. Courgettes come in different colours, and my favourites are the pale green and almost white ones.

Using purple Thai rice give a very unexpected texture, and its colour really complements the opaque pine nut and scarlet pomegranate. Purple Thai rice is available from delicatessens. You can use plain white rice or wild or Camargue rice instead.

8 white courgettes
olive oil
1 onion, finely chopped
2 garlic cloves, minced
salt and pepper
$1/2$ tsp ground allspice
$1/2$ tsp ground cinnamon
180g purple Thai rice
120g pine nuts, toasted
seeds of 2 pomegranates
4 tbsp chopped parsley

To serve
100g Bulgarian feta cheese, cut into chunks

Preheat the oven to 180°C/350°F/Gas 4.

First of all prepare the courgettes. Halve them lengthways then, using a small sharp knife, carefully hollow them out, removing all the seed pulp from the middle.

To make the stuffing heat about 2 tbsp of the olive oil in a large sauté pan and add the onion, garlic, salt, pepper, allspice and cinnamon. Sauté for about 5 minutes, then add the rice and cook for another 2 minutes, making sure that the rice granules are well coated with the spice and nut mixture. Add about 150ml water and cook until the rice is nearly cooked al dente. Add the pine nuts, pomegranate seeds and parsley. Cool.

Fill the courgettes with the stuffing and place in an ovenproof dish. Sprinkle with some olive oil and add some water to the dish. Bake uncovered for about 30 minutes, basting occasionally with the pan juices. Serve with chunks of feta cheese.

COST £9.70

CARDAMOM and POMEGRANATE ROASTED FIGS with POMEGRANATE SABAYON

The fig season is just as brief as the pomegranate season. Get dark purple figs with scarlet red and meltingly soft flesh. Figs, pomegranates and cardamom go beautifully together as they are all reminiscent of warm Mediterranean climates, exotic settings and sweet spices.

8 large figs
30g butter, melted
juice of 2 pomegranates
2 tbsp pomegranate molasses
seeds of 8 cardamom pods, crushed

Sabayon
3 egg yolks
1 tbsp caster sugar
1 tbsp white wine
juice of ½ pomegranate

Preheat the oven to 180°C/350°F/Gas 4.

To prepare the figs, make a cross cut halfway down. Place all eight in a baking tray. Mix together the melted butter, pomegranate juice, molasses and cardamom. Pour this over the figs, and roast in the preheated oven for 15 minutes, basting every now and again with the juices.

Meanwhile place all the ingredients for the sabayon in a heatproof bowl set over simmering water. Cook, whisking constantly, until the mixture has thickened.

To serve, place two figs in each plate and pour over the sabayon.

COST £5.80

THE DRINK SELECTION

This is a warning in advance for those readers alarmed at my colleague's infatuation with particular ingredients (with this menu it is the humble pomegranate). Silvena excitedly rang me just as I was writing the column which comprised this menu, and told me she had just returned from a trip to the Norwegian Arctic Circle where she caught a 70kg cod (in unendangered waters). Steel yourself, brave readers! Cod and cheese soufflé to start, roast cod with cod sauce to follow, and creamed cod rice pudding are surely already brewing in her brain. Easy to deal with, you will remark, and just so. Pomegranates are a different matter.

That pumpkin soup with the blessed fruit is a tricky dish, and it's just for starters. Too many white wines will do little to enhance the dish and I think we need a red, lightly chilled, and this will also carry us over to the stuffed courgettes with their own garnish of pomegranates. My choice of red, then, is **Asda's** own-label **Chilean Merlot 2002**, generously distributed to all branches, and it costs just £2.96 a bottle and rates **16 points**. It offers plums and cherries with a definite spark given it by decent tannins. With the soup, the fruit will lift the pomegranates whilst not disturbing the delicacy of the pumpkin (and with this vegetable in season I make pumpkin soup regularly for guests, adding to it an idea of Michel Roux, the chef who runs the kitchen at Le Gavroche, by garnishing it with brown shrimps). With the main course, the tannins will play more of a role in enhancing the courgettes and melding with the rice. Shall we say three bottles for the four of you?

That's £8.88 gone and a familiar problem recurs: how do we find a wine for £1.02 to go with those figs with pomegranate sabayon? We will cheat. We'll visit **Tesco** and remove **Australia's Finest Botrytis Sémillon 2000** (**16 points**, £4.99 the half bottle) from the shelves and discover a superbly ripe yet gorgeously acidic pud wine of complexity and clout. It will handle those figs as if vinified for no other purpose.

BALSAMIC ROASTED BEETROOT with PANCETTA and BASIL AÏOLI

This is almost worth making for the colours alone. Luckily it tastes good too: the slightly tangy taste of the roasted beetroot with vinegar, allied with the crunchy walnuts, and all dominated by the wonderfully fragrant basil aïoli.

6–8 small beetroots (save any young leaves)
olive oil
4 tbsp balsamic vinegar
125g diced pancetta
100g shelled walnuts
150g rocket leaves

Basil aïoli
2 egg yolks
2 garlic cloves, crushed
2 bunches basil
300ml olive oil
2 tbsp lemon juice
salt and pepper

Boil the beetroots as they are to preserve their extraordinary colour, about 40 minutes. Drain and cover with cold water. Scrub off the skin and cut in half. Place in a oven tray, drizzle with olive oil and roast at 220°C/425°F/Gas 7 until caramelising at the edges, about 15 minutes. Drizzle over the balsamic vinegar and roast for a further 10 minutes.

For the basil aïoli, process the egg yolks, garlic and basil in a food processor to mix well. With the motor still running, gradually add the olive oil in a thin, steady and slow stream until the mixture is thick and glossy. Stir in the lemon juice and season to taste.

Now fry the pancetta in a saucepan over high heat. Add the walnuts and stir over a low heat for 2 minutes. Mix well with the beetroots and cool slightly. Toss with the rocket (and beetroot leaves if using).

To serve, place the beetroot mixture on serving plates, and spoon some of the basil aïoli around and on top.

COST £9.61

PUMPKIN and TOMATO RISOTTO

This is dedicated to real pumpkin lovers like me, the ultimate comfort food presented in the most sensational colours. I was brought up with pumpkin dishes: pumpkin tossed in butter with sage leaves or roasted with rosemary, pumpkin soup, and sweet pumpkin and walnut stuffed filo pastries. When you prepare pumpkin in a savoury dish, season generously as, like all starchy foods, pumpkin needs more salt.

    1 litre vegetable stock (see page 197)
    1 x 440g can plum tomatoes
    3 tbsp olive oil
    3 garlic cloves, finely chopped
    100g butter
    1 large onion, chopped
    500g butternut pumpkin, peeled, seeded and coarsely grated
    300g arborio rice
    salt and pepper
    100g wild rocket
    100g Parmesan cheese, freshly grated

Have the vegetable stock at a simmer in a saucepan near to where you will cook the risotto. Drain the tomatoes, add their juice to the stock and continue to simmer over a low heat.

Heat the oil, add the drained tomatoes and garlic, and cook over a medium heat for 10 minutes until pulpy.

Melt the butter in a large saucepan, add the onion and cook for 5 minutes until soft. Stir in the pumpkin and cook for about 10 more minutes on a medium heat.

Now add the tomato mixture and rice to the pumpkin, and stir. Slowly begin adding the hot stock, a ladleful or cupful at a time, and cook until absorbed, stirring all the time. Add more stock and again stir until absorbed, still stirring constantly, and keep doing so until all the stock has been absorbed. Cook until the rice is tender and creamy, adding more stock or water if necessary.

Season to taste and add the rocket while the rice is still steaming hot. Add the grated Parmesan, and mix gently. Serve immediately with more freshly grated Parmesan.

COST £4.81

LEMON and ALMOND CAKE

One of the best cakes you will ever have, and it's wheat free as well! The original recipe was made with oranges, but I think that lemons work even better; they contribute mind-blowing citrus fragrance and the most stunning colour. The cake will slightly sink in the middle when out of the oven and cooling, but that is quite normal and only adds to the rustic character of the cake.

2 large seedless lemons
unsalted butter for greasing
6 eggs
240g caster sugar
1 tbsp baking powder
240g ground almonds

Wash and scrub the lemons and boil them whole in water to cover for about 1 hour or until soft. Cool before you place them in the food processor and work to a purée.

Preheat the oven to 190°C/375°F/Gas 5. Butter a 24cm springform cake tin and line the bottom with baking paper.

Beat the eggs and sugar for at least 5 minutes until very thick, creamy and volumised, then fold in the baking powder, ground almonds and lemon purée until evenly combined.

Pour the cake mixture into the prepared tin and bake for 45 minutes until firm to the touch. Some ovens make take longer so bake a little longer if the cake still feels wet.

Cool and serve!

COST £4.40

THE WINE SELECTION

There is a marvellously intimidating quality to Silvena's dishes (the starters especially), where no quarter is offered or given. The palate is both soothed and tantalised. Fine for the palate of the diner, not so straightforward for the wine-waiter. What goes with that first course which will combat the richness of aïoli-drenched beetroots? The answer is a highly aromatic (and not cheap) white wine from Alsace made from the Gewürztraminer grape – and Tesco, Sainsbury's, and Safeway each has a splendid wine-co-op sourced 1999 or 2000 vintage at £5.99. However, **Sainsbury's** own-label **Australian Colombard/ Chardonnay 2001** (£2.99) is cheerfully crisp and lip-smackin', and would go with the starter. Later vintages, the 2002 and even the 2003 (not to mention 2004) will also, in my opinion, be fine here even though in the latter vintage the grapes have only been picked this year.

An interesting red for the risotto is **Campo Lindo Crianza Pla de Bages Tempranillo/Cabernet Sauvignon 1997** (Aldi, £2.99). This offers delicious chocolate fruit with a fully mature, velvety richness. It is an amazing bargain from a retailer whose doors few wine-drinkers think of entering. If you buy two bottles, this leaves just £1.03 for a wine to go with Silvena's scrumptious pudding. Clearly impossible, surely? The answer is: not quite. All you need to do is purchase a bottle of **Moscatel de Valencia** (less than £3.99 at all major supermarkets) and offer a small glass of it to each of the four diners. The remainder of the wine can be re-sealed and drunk within the next few days (the bottle will keep perfectly in the fridge). Of course this is a monstrous piece of cheating on my part, but what else can I do? The real answer to this problem is not to have any dessert wine since it will always be impossible to fund three bottles of wine plus a fourth for the pud for a tenner. I shall carry on cheating in this way with many more of Silvena's menus to come (and already have done indeed). Price no object? Then go for a **Monbazillac**, the sweet wine from the Dordogne, or a **Barsac** from Bordeaux.

NORWEGIAN HADDOCK and PRAWN SOUP, served with EMMENTAL CHEESE CROÛTONS

This is a beautifully clear and intensely flavoured soup. I have used Norwegian wild haddock and prawns. The fish is chunky with big juicy flakes; the prawns are tiny pink, sweet jewels, the best cold-water prawns that you can get. Ask your fishmonger to obtain them for you. It really makes all the difference if you are using Norwegian fish as it is of superior quality and taste. Since the prawns are already cooked and in brine, then you need to just add them at the very end.

25g butter
1 onion, finely chopped
1 x 2cm piece fresh root ginger, grated
finely grated zest of 1 lemon
½ tsp cumin seeds
1 litre good fish stock (see page 198)
5 fresh lime leaves
salt and pepper
200g Norwegian haddock fillet, in bite-sized pieces
200g peeled, cooked Norwegian prawns

Croûtons
8 small slices French bread
8 thin slices Emmental cheese

Melt the butter in a large pan, add the onion, ginger, lemon zest and cumin, and cook over a low heat for 3 minutes. Add the fish stock and lime leaves, bring to the boil and simmer for 15 minutes. Season to taste.

Add the haddock and prawns and simmer for 2–3 minutes.

Top the bread slices with cheese and place under a hot grill until the cheese starts to melt. Ladle the soup into bowls and serve with the grilled cheesy croûtons.

COST £4.80

NORWEGIAN ROAST COD with BROAD BEAN and SPINACH POTATO MASH

This dish continues this menu's eco-friendly theme! Cod from the North Sea, so we are told, is nearing extinction, but if you buy cod from the waters of the Norwegian coast and Barents Sea, then you will be able to eat this wonderful fish guilt-free. Norwegian wild cod comes from sustainable fish stocks and is an excellent alternative to the endangered cod species from elsewhere.

1kg floury potatoes
300g frozen broad beans
200g fresh spinach
4 spring onions, chopped
2 garlic cloves, chopped
olive oil
100ml milk
60g butter
4 x 150g pieces Norwegian cod fillet
Maldon salt

To garnish (optional)
40g black pudding, thickly sliced and cooked
20g frozen broad beans, cooked
40g girolle mushrooms, cleaned and pan-fried

Preheat the oven to 200°C/400°F/Gas 6.

Peel the potatoes and boil until soft. Cook the beans and spinach, then drain and purée together until smooth. Fry the spring onion and garlic to soften in about 1 tbsp olive oil, then add the broad bean and spinach purée. Keep warm.

Mash the soft potatoes and add the milk and butter. Stir in the bean and spinach mixture. Keep warm until ready to use.

Pan-fry the cod in about 2 tbsp olive oil over a high heat, about 2 minutes each side. Season with Maldon salt, and put in the preheated oven for 8 minutes.

To serve, spoon the potato mash on to the centre of the plate, and place the cod on top, skin up. If using, garnish with chunks of black pudding, beans and girolles.

COST £ 12.40

QUINCE and GINGER GRANITA

Granita is an Italian coarse-textured frozen water ice. Granita should be truly grainy in texture and not sticky and compact like badly cooked rice pudding. Using quince and ginger is a great seasonal combination. Cypriot or Turkish quinces are also available but these are a pale shadow of the British quince, so do whatever necessary to obtain British quince in order to get the perfect aroma and taste that is like no other.

    2 medium quinces
    250ml sugar syrup (see page 200)
    1 x 2cm piece fresh root ginger, peeled and finely chopped
    500ml water

Peel, quarter and core the quinces. Put the fruit in a saucepan with the sugar syrup and ginger. Boil to start with, and then simmer for 40–60 minutes. Liquidise hot and sieve through a fine sieve. Stir in the water, and leave to cool.

Place in a shallow plastic box, cover and freeze. For granita you need to achieve separate ice crystals so you will need to beat the liquid with a fork at regular intervals during freezing. Start beating after an hour of freezing time, then again every 30 minutes for a total of $2^{1}/2$ hours.

The mixture should be a smooth consistency of identifiable ice crystals. Serve immediately in tall glasses.

COST £ 1.80

THE WINE SELECTION

Silvena says this is her 'Norwegian eco-friendly, guilt-free seafood menu'. Guilt-free? Perhaps for Norwegians. Doubtless for Bulgarian chefs. But not for the pitiful prole who has to choose the wines. What normal mortal can find a wine to accompany haddock and prawn soup which includes ginger, cumin and lime leaves (plus Emmental croûtons, my life) with the budget I'm on? I'm tempted to say the hell with it and just chill to nigh-freezing two bottles of any supermarket own-label fino sherry (Tio Pepe is way out of my league and is in no way superior to the own-label bottles at supermarkets). **Sainsbury's** for starters (sorry, couldn't resist that) has an excellent **Pale Dry Fino**, rating **16 points**, costing £4.49, and so do **Somerfield** (£3.99 and called **Espinosa de los Monteros**) and **Waitrose**. **Tesco's 16-point Finest Fino** is excellent at £4.99. Cheaper is **Montilla** (once part of the sherry region) and **Waitrose's**, at £3.49, literally crackles with **16-point** dry fruit (if it can be characterised as such). Realistically, I guess a half bottle will do for the four of you, a small glass beside each plate, and this will enhance this splendid, otherwise guilt-free soup. The roasted Norwegian cod to follow requires an unfortified white wine, though, and may I suggest two

bottles of **Asda's** non-vintage **Chardonnay, Vin de Pays du Jardin de la France (15.5 points, £2.98)**? This is a superbly simple, citrussy, keen, refreshing white of surprising class. A true cod piece if ever I tasted one.

Now by my reckoning we have spent about £8, and thus we can't really afford to find something exciting for that quince and ginger granita (no cod there, thank the Lord). But I cheat again. I reckon a visit to **Majestic** is called for to find **Pedro Ximénez Viejo Napoleon Hidalgo (18 points, £8.99)**. Its toffee apple and crème brûlée aroma leads to chocolate molasses with butterscotch and a slick, oily, sweet, honied toffee on the finish.

FRESH FIGS, GORGONZOLA and SERRANO HAM

The inspiration for this simple, but hugely colourful and unpretentious dish derives from my carefree Bulgarian childhood. At the back of our home we had a fig orchard, and I would wait until the figs were ripe and swallow them greedily. Figs are irresistibly delicious; choose ripe ones, which will be fragile but hopefully not too damaged while having travelled from source. For dark purple, velvety and juicy figs, with deep red and moist flesh, you will have to pay a bit, but it is definitely worth it! You may notice that this particular starter has a rather high price in comparison with an average one from the book.

    4 very ripe figs, halved
    small bunch of basil leaves
    250g Italian Gorgonzola cheese, creamy and mature
    8 slices ciabatta bread, toasted
    8 slices Serrano ham, very thinly sliced
    olive oil
    salt and pepper

To serve, place two fig halves on each plate. Scatter the basil over the figs. On the side, spoon a dollop of the creamy Gorgonzola and a slice or two of ciabatta. Place the slices of ham between the figs and the cheese, and finally drizzle with some olive oil, salt and pepper.

COST £8.15

LUXURIOUS HADDOCK FISHCAKES with WILTED SPINACH

The average fishcake out there is prepared with plenty of potato for two reasons: it is more cost-effective, but it is also easier to handle and cook as the potato binds all the ingredients better. The result is a bland and uniform mass of starchy and heavy 'fish' cake. Here is a very special version. They are potato free, and really live up to their name.

50g gherkins
50g capers
2 shallots, chopped
finely grated lemon zest
1 egg
600g fresh haddock, skinned and boned
small bunch of coriander, finely chopped
Tabasco sauce to taste
Worcestershire sauce to taste

To cook and serve
50g plain flour
2 eggs, beaten
150g fresh breadcrumbs
vegetable oil for shallow-frying
250g fresh spinach, washed
herbs to garnish (flat-leaf parsley, basil etc.)

Place the gherkins, capers, shallot, lemon zest and egg in a food processor and process until mixed. Add the fish fillet and, using the pulse button, work to a paste. Do not over-process or you will end up with a creamy purée rather than a workable paste. Add the chopped coriander, Tabasco and Worcestershire sauces. Shape into four large rounds and place in the fridge for 30 minutes to set.

To cook, lightly flour each fishcake then dip in the egg mix, followed by the breadcrumbs. Shallow-fry in some oil until golden brown on a medium heat.

Meanwhile, sweat the spinach leaves in just a drop of water for a minute until wilted. Spoon a little of spinach on to the middle of the plate, set a fishcake on the top and garnish with some herbs.

COST £7.36

VANILLA PANNACOTTA with PASSIONFRUIT

A classic all-time favourite dessert, which is very simple and cost-effective to make, but few people dare to cook it. It is over-rated and overly expensive in restaurants but it really is just cooked cream. It's always a safe bet to accompany pannacotta with citrus fruits, and the combination here – the velvety creaminess of the pannacotta with sharp and crunchy passionfruit – is beautiful.

> 1 vanilla pod
> 450ml double cream
> 90g caster sugar
> 1 gelatine leaf
>
> *To serve*
> 2 passionfruit, halved, flesh and seeds squeezed out

Split the vanilla pod sideways across the middle. Scrape the tiny seeds out of the pod, add to the double cream along with the pod, and heat together. Add the sugar and bring to the boil. As soon as it has reached boiling stage, turn off the heat and allow it to infuse for 20 minutes.

Place the gelatine leaf in a bowl of cold water, where it will soften but not dissolve. Heat the cream briefly and remove the vanilla pod. Take the gelatine leaf out of the cold water and gently squeeze to get rid of excess water. Add it to the hot cream then, as soon as the gelatine has dissolved completely, pour the mixture into four ramekin dishes and place in the fridge overnight.

When you are ready to serve the dessert, remove the set creams from the ramekins by briefly placing each ramekin in a bowl of very hot water. The heat will loosen the sides. Invert each ramekin on to the middle of a plate. I find the easiest way of achieving this is to place the dessert plate on top of the ramekin and flipping over, so that the dessert plate is on the bottom. Then gently lift off the ramekin. The result is one slightly wobbly and delicate pannacotta, hopefully in the middle of your plate.

Serve each pannacotta with some squeezed passionfruit flesh and seeds drizzled around the edge.

Cost £3.81

THE WINE SELECTION

Goodness me, how we need something a touch tropical and ripe in a wine to cope with that first course. Gorgonzola is a rich blue cheese and sweet white wines can be marvellous with such cheeses, but in this case its effects are somewhat mollified by the other ingredients. My first choice for this course is, then, **Sainsbury's** non-vintage **California Colombard/Chardonnay**. This rates **15 points** at its normal £3.49 but in promotions its price can be reduced to £2.79 and its rating, in such circumstances if they apply, is upped to **16**. The fruit is on the dry side but it is chewy with a distinct undertone of Alphonso-mango richness and ripeness. You could even splash out on two bottles of this wine. Other wines which will work with the dish include **German Auslesen** and **Alsatian Tokay-Pinot Gris**. I would also like to see how a red with a sweet edge would work because the Serrano ham does give it an interesting nuance which would lend assistance to such a wine. An **Amarone** or **Valpolicella Classico Passito** from northern Italy would be my first choice here, and also interesting would be a sparkling **Shiraz** from Australia (**Banrock Station** is the most widely distributed, around £8). Indeed, I think a red bubbly would be the most entertaining wine choice of all, and it would certainly cause comment around your dinner table.

Next question is what to have with that luxurious fishcake? Oh, how that lemon zest and Tabasco sauce decree that we require something feisty in the fruit of the wine which shall successfully accompany it. Shall we go for a red wine? I drink a lot of red wine with fish and **Tesco's** non-vintage **Corbières** (**16 points**, £2.99) is a snip. It parades fresh plums, cherries and blackcurrants with soft velvety tannins. Unless you are cavalier with the Tabasco in the cake, this wine will be fine. If you'd prefer white wine then I suggest **Hungarian Irsai Oliver 2001** (**Safeway**, **15.5 points**, £2.99) which has floral-edged, gently Muscat-tangy fruit. This is a delicate wine to some extent, so exuberant use of the Worcestershire sauce will be disastrous.

With dessert I recommend **Sainsbury's** non-vintage half bottle of **Muscat de St Jean de Minervois** (**16 points**, £3.79) which is one of the great bargain sweeties on any supermarket wine shelf. A small glass is sufficient, for it flaunts apricots, walnuts and Greek honey with a touch of thyme.

CHARD PARCELS stuffed with SWEET POTATO and WILD RICE

This is very similar to the stuffed vine leaves that we have back home in Bulgaria. We often use spinach, but with the abundance of fresh seasonal chard, there is no excuse but to head to your nearest farmers' market and get some. Chard is excellent for wrapping, better than either vine leaves or spinach. Preferably choose smallish chard leaves with thin stalks, but if you are only able to get large leaves, then cut the stalk out and use the two half leaves to make two parcels.

    200g sweet potatoes, peeled
    salt and pepper
    80g wild rice
    olive oil
    1 shallot, finely chopped
    2 garlic cloves, finely chopped
    1 small red chilli, seeded and finely chopped
    20g plump golden sultanas
    1/4 tsp ground allspice
    8–10 chard leaves, blanched then cooled in cold water

Boil the sweet potatoes, drain and mash them, then season to taste. Meanwhile boil the wild rice: this will take you about 30 minutes, as wild rice takes a lot longer to cook. Drain and keep aside.

Heat about 1 tbsp oil in a frying pan and cook the shallot, garlic, chilli and sultanas for a minute. Add the rice. Stir all this into the sweet potato mash, along with the allspice.

Preheat the oven to 180°C/350°F/Gas 4.

To stuff the blanched chard leaves, lay a leaf on a work surface and place a spoon of mix at the end nearest to you. Roll up, tucking the sides in as well at the same time. Do not be tempted to over-fill the chard parcels. Repeat with the rest of the chard, leaving two leaves only.

Place these remaining leaves on the bottom of a heavy oven dish, sprinkle with olive oil than put in the stuffed chard leaves. Pour in enough water to come halfway up the parcels. Cover with a lid and cook in the preheated oven for about 30 minutes. Serve while hot with some cooking juices.

COST £3.10

ROAST PHEASANT stuffed with BLACK BARLEY, GOLDEN SULTANAS and GINGER

Pheasants are fairly mild in flavour, unlike other game. They are quite plentiful in the autumn and inexpensive: expect to pay £4–5 per bird. A hen will feed two to three people, and a cock three to four people. This recipe uses two cocks, so the helpings are very generous and for the very hungry. The stuffing has a multi-layered, knobbly texture and appearance. Black barley is a most exciting grain and not the easiest to get hold of. You can use pearl barley or Camargue rice instead.

> 2 cock pheasants, ready to cook
> 80g butter
> salt and pepper
>
> *Stuffing*
> 200g black barley
> 2 tbsp olive oil
> 1 shallot, finely chopped
> 80g golden sultanas
> 2 tbsp chopped parsley
> 2 spheres stem ginger, chopped
> juice and finely grated zest of ½ lemon

Cook the barley in some hot water for about 20 minutes, until soft. Drain and keep aside.

Heat the oil in a heavy frying pan, and cook and stir the shallot, sultanas and cooked black barley for a few minutes. Add the parsley, ginger, zest and lemon juice. Cool. When cold, stuff into the cavity of the pheasants and seal up the openings with wooden cocktail sticks.

Meanwhile, preheat the oven to 180°C/350°F/Gas 4.

Smear the birds with butter, sprinkle with salt and pepper to taste, and roast for about an hour, basting at regular intervals. Carve and serve with the stuffing.

COST £12.30

STICKY BLACK THAI RICE PUDDING
with CARAMELISED BANANAS

This is a version of a recipe in *A Cook's Guide to Grains* by Jenni Muir, and is just the perfect winter dessert. Black Thai rice is certainly a lot more interesting than plain pudding rice; it has long, elegant grains and a delicious flavour.

40g butter
100g sticky black rice
340ml coconut milk
100ml cow's milk
120g caster sugar

Caramelised bananas
4 large bananas, peeled and halved
40g butter
6 tbsp maple syrup

Melt the butter in a suitable saucepan, add the rice, and stir to coat. Add the coconut milk, cow's milk and sugar, and stir to combine. Bring to the boil, immediately reduce the heat, cover, and cook on a low heat for about 10 minutes. Keep warm.

To prepare the bananas, heat the butter and sauté the banana halves until slightly browned. Add the maple syrup to coat the bananas well.

Serve the warm sticky black Thai rice pudding, accompanied by the bananas with their juices.

COST £3.40

THE WINE SELECTION

It behoves me to make one thing clear. My contribution to this book is to find sufficient wine for four people, ten quid or under all in. Beer is out. However, one reader did e-mail me and say I should try beer. This, to my palate at least, is a feeble idea. Beer does little to enhance most food, especially spicy, complex dishes (which Silvena's often are), and I do not find it as digestible with food as wine is. Besides, who'd swap a wine waist for a beer belly?

Perish the thought, and let me find a wine for that starter of chard parcels. We shall open with a bottle of **Asda's** own-label non-vintage **Bordeaux Blanc (15.5 points, £2.98)** which shows fresh gooseberryish fruit sufficient to tackle the spices in the dish without wincing. The pheasant requires a bolshie red, virile and firm, and again I'm going for an **Asda** bottle (or rather two bottles). This is the **South African Red (16 points, £2.81)** which offers cherries and roast berries, smoked nuts, and fluent tannins. It should be more than a match for that bird.

That scrumptious rice pudding with caramelised bananas, left with £1.40 left in the kitty to vinously accommodate it, is a bitch but let's exceed the brief, and all expectations, and sink £7.49 on a half bottle of **Campbells Rutherglen Muscat (16.5 points, Somerfield)**. That pud and that wine really are a match, made not in clichéd heaven, but in Thailand and Australia respectively.

But that's only one way of handling this menu. What if money was no object? Let us suppose old Uncle Bartholemew dies by falling asleep and drowning in his bowl of truffle soup. He leaves you his First Editions library, valued by Bertram Rota at £250,000, but only if you spend fabulous sums on wine, only European wine mind (Uncle Bart was mightily old-fashioned), for a dinner party with this the menu. Immediately you telephone Richard Kihl (01728 454455)

or email him (sales@richardkihl.ltd.uk) in Aldeburgh in Suffolk.
Would not an old Madeira of Uncle Bartholomew's birth year, 1911,
be de rigueur? Richard has Bual Blandy Madeira 1911, at £180 the
bottle, and splendid it is with its rich cooked fruit intact and its
acidity still amazingly fresh. He is also able to flog you a case of 1963
Fonseca Port (£1650) to go with the cheese, and Baron de Sigognac
Bas Armagnac 1923 (£350 the bottle) to go with the coffee. However,
for the white wine to go with the first course and for the red to
accompany the pheasant, we must shop elsewhere. The white has to
be Domaine Niellon Chevalier Montrachet 2000 (£2,025 the case at
Fine & Rare Wines, 0208 960 1995, wine@frw.co.uk), and the red
for the pheasant has to be Barbaresco Sori San Lorenzo Angelo Gaja
1995 (£165 the bottle), available at Volvona & Crolla in Edinburgh.

Oh yes, Uncle Bart made one other stipulation: you have to invite
me.

CELERIAC, SWEET POTATO and APPLE SOUP

This is a perfect autumn soup with just the right degree of sweetness. Celeriac gives a wonderfully fulfilling texture, and velvety smooth taste. Celeriac and celery are two very different vegetables, and they mustn't be confused. Celeriac is mostly used in mashes, with potatoes or cauliflower. The apple here adds a slight fruitiness, and goes particularly well with the celeriac.

vegetable oil
a little butter
1 onion, chopped
4 garlic cloves, chopped
1 large orange-fleshed sweet potato, peeled and chopped
300g celeriac, peeled and chopped
1 Granny Smith apple, chopped
salt and pepper

To garnish
crème fraîche

Heat a little oil and some butter in a large soup pot, add the onion and garlic and cook until soft but not brown. Add the chopped potato, celeriac and apple and about 600ml water (or chicken stock if handy). Bring to the boil and simmer gently for 20–30 minutes until the vegetables are soft.

Adjust the seasoning to your liking and blend the soup in a blender or liquidiser. If it is too thick add some more water and again check the seasoning.

Serve hot with a spoonful of crème fraîche on each portion.

COST £2.10

POMEGRANATE-GLAZED DUCK with SAUTÉED PAK-CHOY and BRAISED RHUBARB

This splendidly seasonal dish, with its stunning colours and daring combination of flavours, should set Malcolm a bit of a challenge! The clear, refreshing flavour of pomegranate molasses perfectly accents the plump, luscious meat of the duck breast. The tart sweetness of the rhubarb provides an additional kick, bringing all the flavours to life. Pomegranate molasses is a syrup, which is available in the speciality section of most major supermarkets and in good delicatessens.

> 3 tbsp pomegranate molasses
> finely grated zest of 2 lemons
> 4 duck breasts, trimmed, about 140g each, skin scored
> *To serve*
> 4 rhubarb stalks, cut into 2.5cm diagonal pieces
> 30g butter
> 1 x 2.5cm piece fresh root ginger, peeled
> 1/2 tsp caster sugar
> 225ml chicken stock (made with a cube)
> 200g pak-choy
> salt and pepper
> seeds from 1 pomegranate

Mix together the pomegranate molasses and lemon zest. Rub into the duck breasts and leave overnight.

To prepare the rhubarb, place the butter, piece of ginger, the rhubarb, sugar and two-thirds of the stock in a medium pan and cook over a low to medium heat until the rhubarb is tender. Remove from the heat and take out the ginger. To make a sauce, purée one-third of the rhubarb and some of the cooking liquid until smooth.

Place the duck breasts in a very hot, heavy-bottomed pan, skin-side down. Cook for 4–8 minutes on each side, or until the skin is golden brown and crisp, and the duck is cooked to medium. Once the breasts are browned on the outside you can reduce the heat to medium to finish cooking for perhaps about 5 more minutes on each side. You can also place the duck in a hot oven to finish cooking for about 10 more minutes.

Allow the duck to rest for a few minutes, and then thinly slice. Reserve any cooking juices. Add the pak-choy to the pan and quickly wilt with the remaining stock. Season to taste.

To serve, place some pak-choy on to the middle of the plate and arrange the duck slices around. Top the duck with the rhubarb pieces and spoon some rhubarb sauce and duck juices around the plate. Sprinkle with fresh pomegranate seeds.

COST £12.92

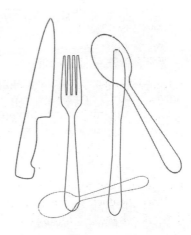

CHOCOLATE MACADAMIA BROWNIE

There are so many recipes for chocolate brownies and yet it is very difficult to find a moist, chewy and hugely chocolatey brownie. I think I've cracked it! This one is rich and intense, suitably impressive for a dinner party. The quality of the chocolate is very important, though, and 70 per cent cocoa solids chocolate is vital. Macadamia nuts are a very luxurious addition – they are crunchy and creamy at the same time – but you could try using other nuts such as pecans or hazelnuts. It is imperative to slightly under-cook the brownie, rather than over-cook it, for that chewy and moist texture.

125g unsalted butter, diced
125g dark chocolate (70% cocoa solids), broken into pieces
2 eggs
180g caster sugar
125g plain flour
2 tbsp self-raising flour
80g shelled macadamia nuts, chopped

To serve
1 small tub mascarpone cheese

Preheat the oven to 180°C/350°F/Gas 4. Grease a 20cm square cake tin and line the bottom with greaseproof paper.

Place the butter and chocolate in a bowl over a saucepan of simmering water and melt gently, stirring until the mixture is smooth.

Place the eggs and caster sugar in a bowl and beat until pale and thick. Fold in the chocolate mixture, sifted flours and macadamia nuts, and pour the mixture into the prepared tin.

The baking time is very important, and I find that baking them for about 18–20 minutes allows the brownies to remain moist and just slightly under-cooked. If they spend too long in the oven they will end up crumbly (which is also fine if you like a crumbly brownie!). To achieve this, allow 10 more minutes in the oven.

Cool the brownies and cut into squares. There will be more than enough for four people. Serve with a dollop of creamy mascarpone.

Cost £4.70

THE WINE SELECTION

They warned me. I pooh-poohed them. Bulgarian chef? Blonde? Knows how to wield a sharp knife? They said a happy marriage would be impossible. Of course I didn't listen. I like boldness in a chef, I said. I welcome feistiness in the ingredients and the challenge to create a perfect union with the wines. You'll see, they said. Now I do see. This menu really gives the Jeremiahs a field day. How could you do this to me, Silvena? Okay, so celeriac, sweet potato and apple soup isn't too tricky. I suggest a bottle of **Asda's** non-vintage **L'Angelot Vin de Pays Blanc** to go with this. It offers light pear and gooseberry fruit and will be an excellent foil for that starter. It costs £3.47 and rates **16 points**. An alternative idea would be an Aussie **Chardonnay**, one of those big rich buttery productions from South Australia or New South Wales.

Now comes the wicked part. A pomegranate-glazed duck breast is a tricky beast at the best of times but since this one is also sautéed with pak-choy and braised rhubarb, there are further hurdles for the wine to jump. I must protest. How can I find the perfect wine for such a (admittedly scrumptious) dish on my budget? The wine I would prefer to serve, regardless of cost, would be a sensational Alsatian: **Domaine Zind-Humbrecht Gewürztraminer Wintzenheim Vieilles Vignes 1999** (£14.41, **Anthony Byrne Fine Wines**). But I haven't the money for this – and Mr Byrne has other vintages no less fine – and so I'm going to have to plump, and plump is the word, for two bottles of **Somerfield's South African Red** (£3.29 x 2 at **16 points**). This leaves me 5p over budget and nothing with which to accommodate that truly amazing chocolate-macadamia brownie. Well, if you don't mind splurging I suggest you buy, since you are shopping at **Somerfield**, a 50cl bottle of **Muscat de Frontignan** (£4.29). It is liquid honied heaven (just like the pud it will so effortlessly lubricate). Of course, given the freedom to roam the shelves I would probably let my hand fall on a Maury, the sweet red wine, highly alcoholic, from Catalan France. **Waitrose** has **Maury Vin Doux Naturel** at 16.5% alcohol in the half bottle (and **16 points**) for £3.99 or £95.76 the 24-bottle case delivered through **Waitrose Direct**.

WINTER

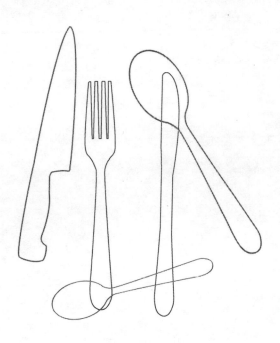

CURRIED SQUASH SOUP with SCALLOPS

Butternuts are plentiful and inexpensive into early winter. Unlike dry pumpkin, butternuts make elegant and velvety soups. Because the butternut base is mellow and creamy, the addition of the spices allows another layer of interest and brings a bite. I would even recommend that if you happened to have some home-made or a good shop-bought curry paste, than add it instead of the curry powder. The scallops are an added luxury, as always.

- 400g butternut squash, peeled, seeded and chopped
- 30g butter
- 1 small onion, chopped
- 4 garlic cloves, chopped
- 1 carrot, chopped
- 1 x 5cm piece fresh ginger root, peeled and grated
- 1 tsp mild Madras curry powder or curry paste
- 1 pear, peeled, cored and cut in small squares
- 250ml vegetable stock (see page 197)
- 100ml coconut milk
- salt and pepper
- juice and finely grated zest of 1 orange
- 4 large scallops
- 50g unsweetened coconut flakes, toasted

Preheat the oven to 200°C/400°F/Gas 6, and bake the butternut for 30 minutes. Heat the butter in a heavy saucepan, add the onion, garlic and carrot, and cook until soft. Add the ginger and curry spice and, after a minute, the cooked squash and the pear. Stir for another minute, then slowly pour in the stock. Simmer uncovered for 30 minutes.

Cool and purée in a blender. Return to a gentle heat and add the coconut milk. Season to taste, and finish with the juice and zest of the orange.

To serve, sauté the scallops in a very hot heavy frying pan or cast-iron griddle pan for a minute or two on each side. Pour the soup and add a scallop and a sprinkling of coconut flakes to each portion.

COST £5.20

ROAST PARTRIDGE with CARAMELISED PEARS, SOUR CHERRIES and WILTED CHARD

Partridges are small birds, the hen weighing about 400g and the cock about 425g. At this time of year you can get them in good supermarkets, but to be confident that they are of the freshest quality, than head to your local farmers' market. Partridge goes very well with another seasonal ingredient, pears. I have also added plump semi-dried cherries, but you can stay true to the season and use cranberries instead. The balsamic jelly is new, and delicious, and sadly rare: if you can't find it, use a cherry jelly or any berry jelly.

    2 small hen partridges
    about 60g butter
    salt and pepper
    2 large shallots, chopped
    3 pears, peeled, cored and sliced
    50g semi-dried cherries
    4 juniper berries, crushed
    2 tsp balsamic jelly (see above)
    300g chard, washed and trimmed

Preheat the oven to 200°C/400°F/Gas 6.

Rub about a third of the butter over the birds, and season with salt and pepper. Cover with foil and place in the preheated oven for about 40 minutes. Remove the foil and roast for another 30 minutes, having increased the temperature of the oven to 240°C/475°F/Gas 9. Baste frequently. When ready, allow to rest for about 15 minutes.

Meanwhile, in a frying pan, sweat the shallots in half the remaining butter until softened, then add the sliced pears and the cherries and cook slowly until the fruits begin to caramelise. Add the juniper berries, balsamic jelly and cooking juices from the roast partridges. Keep warm.

While the partridges are resting, sauté the chard in the rest of the butter until just wilted.

Serve the partridges, accompanied by the caramelised pears and cherries and wilted chard.

COST £11.50

OLIVE OIL and DATE CAKE

This is a very simple and flavoursome cake. Adding olive oil makes it very moist and fragrant. The dates I have used are the soft semi-dried ones. It is well worthwhile trying to get the best possible quality of dates. Add some pecans if you want a crunch.

    250ml best-quality extra virgin olive oil
    4 eggs, separated
    300g caster sugar
    400g plain flour
    2 tsp baking powder
    200ml crème fraîche
    50ml milk
    100g pitted semi-dried dates, chopped

Preheat the oven to 180°C/350°F/Gas 4, and use a little of the olive oil to grease a 26cm springform cake tin.

Whip the egg yolks and sugar together until thick and creamy, then slowly add the oil. Pour in the flour and baking powder and mix well. Add the crème fraîche, milk and dates and incorporate well.

Whip the egg whites and slowly and carefully fold into the cake mixture. Pour into the prepared tin and bake in the preheated oven for about 50 minutes. Leave to cool in the tin before unclipping the tin.

Serve cold in wedges with a dollop of crème fraîche.

COST £3.50

THE WINE SELECTION

The myriad flavours of curried butternut squash soup with scallops and toasted coconut (a soup, furthermore, containing a fair slug of ginger, Madras curry powder, coconut milk and orange peel) require a crisp white wine of character and bite. With the next course we are faced with a bird accompanied by caramelised pears and sour cherries. A formidable set of opponents against which **Somerfield** has two absurdly cheap, **16-point** own-label Chilean wines to go with that saucy soup as well as that frisky bird. **Sauvignon Blanc 2003** (£3.99) shows elegant citrus and peach. **Cabernet Sauvignon 2002** (£4.03) has bright plums, some lively blackcurrant edging, and surprisingly stylish tannins. The Sauvignon has just the right balance of freshness with an elegant citrussiness to take on the soup, and the Cabernet takes itself seriously enough to get along with the partridge as well as being sufficiently relaxed, fruity, and easygoing not to be overcome by the pears and cherries. All in all, then, as usual in the way this book orders its world, a feast for peanuts.

The date cake? Sorry, squire, madam, not enough in the kitty. A bottle of Sauvignon for the soup and two bottles of the Cabernet for the bird leaves us having overspent, but it's all in a good cause. Money no object? Then go for the wine I recommended in autumn's menu 9, **Campbells Rutherglen Muscat** (**16.5 points**, £7.49 the half bottle, **Somerfield**). A date with that cake is just what this molasses-rich Australian is crying out for.

ROASTED PEAR and FENNEL SALAD
with SHALLOT VINAIGRETTE

Pears, the ultimate winter fruit, infused with the aroma of rosemary and combined with roasted fennel, create this wonderful and flavourful salad. Pears are one of the best seasonal British fruit, and for freshness are best sourced from small growers and farmers' markets.

80g pecan nut halves
2 medium pears, peeled, cored and halved
4 sprigs rosemary
1 medium fennel bulb, cored and sliced 3mm thick lengthways
olive oil
salt and pepper
200g mixed salad leaves, washed and dried

Shallot vinaigrette
20ml red wine vinegar
1 shallot, finely grated
40ml olive oil
1/2 tsp any mustard

Preheat the oven to 180°C/350°F/Gas 4. Roast the pecans for 5 minutes. Remove and cool.

Spear each pear half with a rosemary sprig and place on a baking sheet. Put the fennel on a separate baking sheet. Brush the pears with olive oil, season with some salt and pepper and bake in the preheated oven for 40 minutes, or until tender. After 20 minutes, brush the fennel with some olive oil and season to taste, then roast alongside the pears for 20 minutes, or until soft and lightly golden. Remove both trays from the oven, and set aside to cool, discarding the rosemary.

To make the vinaigrette, mix all the ingredients in a small bowl.

When the pears are cool, cut each half into 3mm slices. In a large bowl mix the salad leaves with the fennel and pear. Pour the shallot vinaigrette over the salad and toss gently to combine. Place the salad mixture in the centre of each plate and garnish with the roasted pecans.

COST £5.40

THAI CHICKEN and PUMPKIN CURRY

A mild dish, with its principal ingredients simmered gently in a thin coconut sauce, then finished with the enlivening flavours of fresh ginger, turmeric, lemongrass and coriander. This curry is easy on the palate, but fragrant and oozing flavours. Pumpkin takes particularly well to spices and is always an excellent addition to curries. Leave out the chicken, and instead add tofu or pak-choy, and you have a vegetarian version. Serve with plain boiled rice.

- 3 tbsp vegetable oil
- 1 onion, chopped
- 2 garlic cloves, chopped
- 1 x 7.5cm piece fresh root ginger, peeled and finely chopped
- 1 x 5cm piece fresh turmeric, peeled and finely chopped
  (or ½ tsp turmeric powder if unavailable)
- 1 tbsp yellow Thai curry paste
- 250ml chicken stock (see page 197)
- 1 x 440ml can coconut milk
- 6 kaffir lime leaves, fresh or dry
- 3 fresh lemongrass stalks, halved lengthways
- 4 chicken fillets, skin removed and cut into chunks
- 120g peeled and seeded pumpkin, cut into chunks
- small bunch of coriander, finely chopped
- 80ml double cream (optional)
- salt and pepper

Heat the oil in a saucepan, add the onion, garlic, ginger and turmeric and cook for 5 minutes on a low heat or until soft. Stir in the curry paste and cook for a further minute. Add the stock, coconut milk, lime leaves and lemongrass, and bring to the boil.

Now add the chicken and pumpkin and simmer gently for 20 minutes or until the chicken is cooked. Discard the lemongrass and add the coriander. Drizzle some cream on top if using. Season to taste.

COST £12.30

PASSIONFRUIT CURD on HAZELNUT PAVLOVA

Passionfruit is a pavlova's best friend, with its intriguing acidic qualities offsetting the sweetness of the meringue: the ultimate culinary power couple! The silky texture of the passionfruit curd breaks through the crusty exterior of the meringue to the marshmallow interior.

4 egg whites
110g caster sugar
100g icing sugar
1 tsp cornflour
1 tsp white wine vinegar
1/2 tsp vanilla extract
40g shelled hazelnuts, finely ground
280ml double cream, lightly whipped

Passionfruit curd
2 eggs, plus 2 extra yolks
inside pulp from 4 passionfruits (wrinkled are the best)
30g butter, finely diced
60g caster sugar

Preheat the oven to 150°C/300°F/Gas 2. Line an oven tray with baking parchment.

For the pavlovas, beat the egg whites with the caster sugar for at least 3 minutes, until very firm. Add the icing sugar, cornflour, vinegar and vanilla, and beat for 4 more minutes until very stiff and glossy. Add the hazelnuts and beat to mix them in.

Spoon the meringue on to the parchment-lined tray in four roughly circular mounds of about 6cm in diameter and about 5cm tall. Reduce the oven heat to 140°C/275°F/Gas 1, and bake the pavlovas for 45 minutes. Once ready, take out and cool.

To make the passionfruit curd, put all the ingredients in a bowl set over a pan of simmering water and stir constantly until the mixture starts to thicken. Continue cooking for about another 10 minutes or until it thickens further, stirring continuously. Remove from the heat, pour the curd into a clean container and let it cool.

To serve, spoon some whipped cream on to each pavlova and pour over it some passionfruit curd.

COST £ 2.30

THE WINE SELECTION

My theory is that Silvena is a reincarnated Lady Macbeth and
therefore hates anyone called Malcolm. Look at that first course. Is it
a friendly gesture to ask me to find a wine to go with roasted pears
and fennel salad with a shallot vinaigrette? A German Riesling
stands some chance and **Bert Simon's Serriger Herrenberg Riesling
Spätlese 1989 (16.5 points, Majestic, £5.99)** should fit the bill, and
whilst you're in the shop take a look at the same producer's
Eitelsbacher Marienholz Riesling Kabinett 1989 (17 points, £4.99)
which would be wonderful to sip as you cook.

The first hurdle cleared, Lady Macbeth throws up a second. A Thai
chicken and pumpkin curry fused with spices and coconut milk will
work nicely with pricey stuff like **New Zealand Sauvignon** (though
the **Serriger Herrenberg** above is certainly a goer). Fresh ginger,
lemongrass and lime leaf with coriander to garnish cry out for the
searing crispness of **Sauvignon** or, may I also say, for the alternative
spicy sweetness of a vibrant **Gewürztraminer. Thresher**, **Sainsbury's**,
Tesco, **Safeway** and **Asda** all have splendid 2000 and 2001 vintage
examples of the latter (**16.5 points, £5.99** to **£6.99**), and they will
enhance the dish as much as the dish will enhance the wine.

I have, I think, well spent my tenner already and so the pavlova, an
Australian conceit named after the Russian ballerina, bristling, note,
with a curd made from the pulp of four passionfruits, is bereft. In
any case, you cannot find for it a vinous partner costing peanuts.
Oh well, hang the expense (and blast these impossible chefs). The
wine to go with the pavlova has got to be **Château d'Yquem 1990**
(**20 points, £120** the half bottle, **Waitrose** at Canary Wharf only).
A hundred and twenty quid for a half bottle! That'll settle her
Ladyship's hash (and her pavlova).

BEETROOT MOUSSE with HORSERADISH CREAM

This wonderful dish is inspired by *The Café Paradiso Cookbook* and is one of the best ways of preparing beetroot. The mousse is as beautiful to look at as it is to eat, and pairing it with horseradish makes a sharp contrast.

vegetable oil for greasing
300g boiled beetroot, peeled
2 garlic cloves
80g cream cheese
juice of 1 small lemon
1 egg plus 1 egg white
40ml double cream
salt and pepper

Horseradish sauce
100g dry mashed potato, made with 125g potatoes
2 tbsp creamed horseradish
40ml double cream
40g butter

Preheat the oven to 180°C/350°F/Gas 4. Oil four ramekins, and place a piece of greaseproof paper on the bottom of each.

Place the beetroot in a food processor with the garlic, cream cheese and lemon juice, and blend to a smooth purée. With the motor running add the egg, then the egg white. Stir in some cream, enough to give a very thick pouring consistency, but not too thick. Season to taste.

Fill the prepared ramekins almost to the top with the mixture, then place them into an oven dish. Pour boiling water in to come halfway up the sides of the ramekins. Cook in the preheated oven until the mousses are firm to the touch, about 45–60 minutes. Let them cool.

To make the horseradish sauce, combine the mashed potato and horseradish in a saucepan over a low heat. Add the cream and butter slowly until you have a mixture the consistency of a thick puréed soup. Season and keep warm.

Serve immediately by turning the mousses out on to serving plates. Spoon the horseradish sauce around the mousses.

COST £2.99

OYSTER MUSHROOMS in GINGERED BUTTER SAUCE, served with PAK-CHOY COLCANNON

Oyster mushrooms, with their subtle, delicate flavour and texture, cook beautifully and, unlike other mushrooms, they don't let their juices out while cooking. Ginger is added at the end so that the flavours are kept sharp and fresh. The mushrooms are served with a traditional Irish colcannon, but with a twist.

> 300g fresh oyster mushrooms, cleaned
> 1 tbsp grated fresh root ginger
> 50g butter, softened
>
> *Pak-choy colcannon*
> 400g mashed potato, made using 600g boiled potatoes
> 50g butter
> 5 tbsp milk
> 200g pak-choy, lightly blanched and chopped
> 1 bunch spring onions, thinly sliced
> 10 slices streaky bacon, cooked to a crisp and chopped
> 2 tbsp finely chopped parsley
> salt and pepper

For the colcannon, make the potato purée while the mashed potatoes are hot. Work in the butter and milk until creamy, then add the pak-choy, spring onion, crisp bacon pieces and parsley. Fold the ingredients through the potato purée and season. Keep the colcannon warm.

To cook the mushrooms, add the ginger to most of the butter and set aside. Melt the rest of the butter in a shallow pan. Add the mushrooms to it, turning them now and again, until lightly browned. This will take around 4 minutes. Now add the gingered butter and take off the heat immediately.

To serve, spoon some pak-choy colcannon into the middle of a plate and place some of the gingered oyster mushroom on top. Drizzle the transparent buttery pan sauces around.

Note

For a vegetarian version you may replace the crisp bacon with crisp tofu.

Cost £10.40

FLOURLESS CHOCOLATE ROULADE with CHESTNUT CREAM

A wheat-free version of a classic dessert! An exceptionally light and chocolatey roulade filled with chestnut-flavoured cream. Chocolate and chestnut are natural partners, complementing each other beautifully. A great dessert for the festive period around Christmas.

150g good cooking chocolate, broken into pieces
5 eggs, separated
175g caster sugar
1 tbsp chestnut purée
300ml double cream, lightly whipped
icing sugar, for dusting

Preheat the oven to 180°C/350°F/Gas 4. Line a 30 x 20cm Swiss roll tin with greased baking paper.

Place the chocolate in a small saucepan sitting over a larger pan with some boiling water. Make sure that the bottom of the small saucepan doesn't touch the boiling water. The chocolate will slowly melt. Leave to cool.

Whisk the egg yolks with the sugar until thick and pale. Fold in the melted chocolate.

In a separate bowl, whisk the egg whites. Fold them carefully into the chocolate mixture, mixing well and making sure you do not over-work the mixture, as you will lose the airy texture.

Spread the mixture into the prepared tin and bake in the preheated oven for about 15 minutes. Make sure that you do not over-cook as this will make the sponge very dry and it will break when you roll it. Leave to cool.

Meanwhile mix the chestnut purée into the cream, making sure it is smooth.

To assemble, turn the roulade out on to another piece of paper dusted with icing sugar and remove the lining paper. Spread the chestnut cream over the roulade. Roll the sponge away from you using the paper to guide you. Trim the ends for a neat finish, but don't worry if it cracks a bit. Chill the roulade and dust with icing sugar before serving.

COST £4.50

THE WINE SELECTION

The trouble with this menu is that I am inclined to start with the pud. Now in fact this was physically accomplished some years ago by a band of daffy gourmets who set out to discover why we order dishes in the way we do and always finish with the sweetest, and so they kicked off with the dessert and when, several dishes later, they came to the oysters at the finish, they were feeling pretty green indeed. I do not, however, propose that we actually eat that gruesomely scrumptious pud first, but that we find some wines for it now and then work backwards. So. With that chocolate roulade I am inclined to go for **Oddbins' Maculan Dindarello** from Italy (£6.99 the half bottle) because I am convinced it is a marriage made in heaven. Another candidate is **Sainsbury's Cranswick Botrytis Sémillon** from Australia (£4.99 the half bottle).

Shall we now say, for the sake of argument, that I have blown half my tenner? C'mon. Be charitable. Okay, so I have a fiver to find wines for the mushroom dish and the beetroot mousse and a good choice is **Asda's** vibrant, sexy, thrusting, dynamic **Dumisani Pinotage/Shiraz** (£3.98) from the Cape (and I must tell you that **South African Pinotage** in general, if it is of the latest vintage, is fine with this dish). Of course you might be inclined to buy three bottles of this wine, and forget all about sweet wines for the dessert, and you would still go over your tenner. Another thought is to visit **Tesco** and choose the own-label **Simply Pinot Grigio** from Hungary (£2.99) to go with the mousse – and rather well it would go too – and then grab two bottles of the same retailer's **Primitivo/Sangiovese** (£3.99) from Italy. Okay, so I'm still over budget. Sue me.

GRATIN of CABBAGE DUMPLINGS

This menu is a homage to The Wolseley, the café-restaurant in London's Piccadilly, with its wonderful mix of Central European café cuisines, a celebration of many things yet to be discovered in the West, with a strong cultural heritage. This is home to me!

Cabbage dumplings are the perfect winter starter, smothered in 'katshkawalj', a Bulgarian cheese made from ewes' milk. Other East European countries also have versions of it. It is available in delis, but you could use mild Cheddar if you can't get hold of the real thing.

2 tbsp vegetable oil
500g Savoy cabbage, grated
1 tbsp runny honey
250g plain flour, plus extra for dusting
25g butter
1 egg, lightly beaten
salt and pepper
80g katshkawalj cheese, grated

Preheat the oven to 180°C/350°F/Gas 4.

Heat the oil in a heavy-based pan, add the cabbage, and sweat for a few minutes until soft. Add the honey and continue stirring until the cabbage is slightly brown. Leave to cool completely.

Meanwhile, place the flour in a bowl, add the butter, egg and a pinch of salt, and mix to a soft dough. Add some water to get the right consistency, about 1–2 tbsp. The dough should be soft and elastic. Roll it out to about 1cm thick on a floured work surface.

Now spread the cool cabbage on to the dough, season with salt and pepper and roll the dough around the cabbage as you would a Swiss roll. Cut the roll into 3–5cm pieces and roll each of these into balls. Have a large saucepan with boiling salted water ready and drop in the dumplings, a few at the time. They are ready as soon as they rise to the top.

Dry and place all the dumplings in a small baking tray. Cover them with grated cheese and bake in the preheated oven for 10 minutes, finishing with 3–5 minutes under the grill to brown.

Cost £3.10

HUNGARIAN GOULASH served with SPÄTZLE

The origins of this dish date back to the ninth century, when nomadic tribes prepared a meal that was suitable for their way of life. They would stew the meat slowly until all the cooking liquid had boiled away, then the meat was dried in the sun, so it could be used at a later time. There are many regional variations, but this is one of the best. Spätzle are small dumplings, made from flour, egg and cream poached in water. The singular word means 'little sparrow' and the dumplings are typical of German and Austro-Hungarian cuisines. Veal is the best meat to use in goulash, but pork is good too.

Sauerkraut is white cabbage that has been finely sliced, salted and fermented. The word means 'bitter herb'. It is a speciality of Alsace and Bavaria, but is very common in Eastern Europe, where households prepare it at home for the winter months.

1kg sauerkraut (available in delis)
2 small onions, chopped
4 tbsp olive oil
800g veal fillet, cut into 1cm cubes
1 tsp salt
1½ tsp paprika
1 large tomato, chopped
1 tsp caraway seeds
4 tbsp buttermilk
125ml soured cream

Spätzle
250g plain flour
2 eggs
2 tbsp double cream
½ tsp salt
¼ tsp freshly ground black pepper
¼ tsp freshly grated nutmeg

To make the goulash, first squeeze the sauerkraut dry. In a heavy-based casserole sauté the onions in the oil until soft, then take them out and keep aside while you brown the veal. Add the onions back to the casserole, along with the salt, paprika, chopped tomato and caraway seeds. Stir well and put the sauerkraut on top.

Pour in enough water to just cover the cabbage, and cover with a lid. Simmer until the meat and cabbage are tender, for at least 25 minutes. Adjust the liquid with more water if needed.

To make the spätzle, mix together the flour, eggs and cream to make a dough, then season with salt, pepper and nutmeg. Have a large saucepan of boiling salted water ready. Shape the dough, using your hands, into small dumplings. Drop them a few at the time into the water. They are ready when they rise to the top. Keep warm.

When the meat is ready , stir in the buttermilk and soured cream. Season to taste and simmer for a few more minutes. Serve the goulash with the spätzle.

COST £13.80

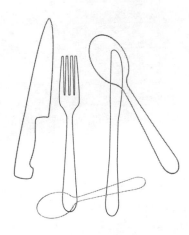

WIDOW'S KISSES

These typical Viennese tea biscuits, with a wonderfully intriguing name, are very easy to make. They are light, crumbly, stuffed with crunchy nuts, rather like luxurious meringues, with a marshmallow texture.

4 egg whites
175g caster sugar
225g shelled pecan nuts, coarsely chopped
115g candied orange peel, finely chopped

Preheat the oven to 120°C/250°F/Gas ¹/₂, and line a baking sheet with baking paper.

Whisk the egg whites and sugar in a bowl sitting over hot water until thick and creamy. Remove from the heat and continue to whisk until cool. Fold in the nuts and peel.

Spoon small rounds of the mixture on to the lined baking sheet and bake in the oven for 15 minutes. Cool and serve with coffee or tea. You will have about 16.

Cost £3.05

THE WINE SELECTION

To say this menu brought a tear to my eye (nothing directly to do
with pepper, nutmeg and paprika) is an understatement. As I weep,
keeping my iMac keyboard dry with paper tissues, the flow is made
all the more touching by the fact that Silvena had no inkling, before
she prepared this menu, of any of my family's culinary history and
its Viennese background. My grandfather, who was the Austrian
Kaiser's barber and a notable dumpling chef on the side, passed on
the latter talent to my father (born in 1899) and this great
sentimentalist and British Army corporal prepared similar dishes to
Silvena's when he cooked for German prisoners of war in the
summer of 1918 (the irony of which we do not need to go into here).
I ate cabbage dumplings for breakfast every morning until the age of
17 (when I was introduced to cornflakes by a sympathetic older
woman in Soho). However, this is the first time I have had to find
wines to go with such things and so if my hand shakes as I pour
please forgive me.

A gratin of cabbage dumplings requires an aromatic white wine, and
if money were no object I would specify an Austrian liquid made
from the Grüner Veltliner grape, but my budget compels me to shop
more rationally and so we shall visit the **Co-op** for the gently spicy
own-label **Argentine Torrontes-Chardonnay 2003 (less than four
quid)**. Now let us turn to the Hungarian goulash with spätzle (which
is from the Swabian, I believe) and I'm sorry to have to modify my
chef's words here but 'sauerkraut' can really only mean acid or acidic
cabbage not bitter herb (though 'kraut', in other contexts, means
'herb' and in Austria a 'Krautler' is a greengrocer). I did not know
this dish had a nomadic origin but it is highly appropriate as we may
have to wander about a bit to find the right red wine. I say red but if
I were to eat the dish at home I'd serve young **Moselle Riesling**, of
Spätlese level, with it but my purse compels restraint and so I

recommend the **Co-op's Vin de Pays d'Oc Cabernet Sauvignon 2002** (sometimes priced at £2.79) which has sufficient fruit. However, you could serve one white wine throughout the meal and for this we visit **Marks & Spencer** for the gorgeous **Domaine Mandeville Viognier 2002/3 (under a fiver)**. As for widow's kisses, which I assume refers to their makers' habit of using them to seduce widowers (or any likely male for that matter), we must surely serve **Tokaji**, the great dessert wine of the Austro-Hungarian empire. **Tesco** has a bottle, of the 1996 vintage, for £9.53. It will push you over budget but it will keep you within the correct boundaries geographically.

CAULIFLOWER SOUP with PESTO SAUCE

A velvety smooth, rich and satisfying winter soup. I have cooked the cauliflower in milk to keep the pure whiteness of it. The flavour and texture are delicate and light, unlike most winter soups.

10g butter
1 shallot, finely chopped
1 medium cauliflower, cut into florets
500ml milk
50ml single cream
salt and pepper
2 tbsp good-quality pesto (see page 200)
olive oil

In a large saucepan melt the butter and sweat the chopped shallot to soften. Add the cauliflower florets and cook for a further 5 minutes on a low to medium heat.

Cover with the milk, bring to boiling point and then immediately reduce to a simmer for about 25 minutes, until the cauliflower is soft. Blend in a food processor, add the cream and some seasoning, and keep warm.

Mix the pesto sauce with about $^1/_2$ tbsp of olive oil to just thin it out.

To serve, pour the soup into bowls and drizzle with some pesto sauce.

COST £3.50

GOAT'S CHEESE, PUMPKIN and SAGE TART, with ORANGE PEPPER SAUCE

This the Cinderella of vegetable tarts! Once cooked, it is almost luminous in colour, and as if the orange-fleshed pumpkin was not enough, we add some more colour and smoothness with the orange pepper sauce, which complements the chalky texture of the goat's cheese.

250g shortcrust pastry
1 large orange pepper
200g mixed salad leaves

Tart filling
200g pumpkin, skinned, seeded and cut into chunks
olive oil
50g butter
2 tbsp sage leaves
150g goat's cheese
3 eggs
200ml double cream
salt and pepper

First of all prepare the tart shell. Roll out the pastry to line a 25cm tart ring and, very gently, use your fingers to press it into shape. Make sure that the pastry is not too soft as it will be very difficult to hold the shape. Trim off excess pastry. Place in the refrigerator for 30 minutes.

Preheat the oven to 180°C/350°F /Gas 4. Cover the pastry-lined ring with a sheet of baking paper and fill with rice or, even better, baking beans if you have some. Blind-bake for 10 minutes, when the pastry will be lightly brown around the edges. Remove from the oven and cool.

Now roast the pumpkin with some olive oil, the butter and some of the sage leaves for about 20 minutes, until soft and just browned. Let the pumpkin cool.

Spread the pumpkin over the base of the par-cooked tart shell. Crumble the goat's cheese evenly over the pumpkin and sprinkle with the rest of the sage leaves. In a bowl, mix the eggs and cream together, and season well. Pour this custard over the tart filling and bake in the oven for about 20 minutes until the filling is set.

To make the pepper sauce, roast the pepper whole in the oven for about 15–20 minutes. Once cool enough to handle, skin the pepper and remove the stalk and seeds. The flesh should be soft but firm. Place the pepper in a food processor to purée, adding a little olive oil to get a slightly runny consistency.

Serve the tart at room temperature or warmed with the orange pepper sauce and a green salad.

COST £8.50

POACHED PEARS in CINNAMON, VANILLA and CITRUS SYRUP

Pears, which are at their best in the winter, are prepared in the company of cinnamon and vanilla – a great flavour combination! I like to use Comice or Conference pears, slightly under-ripe and firm. If they are too ripe, they will have a starchy and floury taste.

juice and zest of 1 large lemon
juice and zest of 1 large orange
250ml water
180g caster sugar
4 cinnamon sticks
1 vanilla pod, split lengthways
4 pears, cored

Place all the ingredients except for the pears in a medium saucepan. Cook gently until the sugar has dissolved and the liquid is starting to simmer.

Peel the pears and place them in the syrup. Cover and cook for about 15 minutes on a medium heat. The syrup should now have slightly thickened. Take out the pears and thinly slice them, keeping the syrup warm.

To serve, place slices of pear in four deep plates and spoon some strained warm syrup over.

COST £3.00

THE WINE SELECTION

Goodness me! I've been working with the woman for many menus now and at last she's being nice to me. Cauliflower soup with pesto? A doddle. That goat's cheese tart? A pushover (even with its pepper sauce). Poached pears? Easy.

The first retailer to consider is **Marks & Spencer**. A red wine of personality and poise is required for both the soup and the tart and I can offer you a choice of two, both available at M & S. **Château du Parc 2001** (£4.99) is a delicious, gently roasted, organic red from the Midi and it is the epitome of rustic civility, characterful yet classy, with deep berries and a hint of feistiness about its tannins. You can simply buy three bottles of this **16-point** wine and that's your dinner party taken care of. I would bank on later vintages of this wine also (though I have not tasted them). Alternatively, for the red wine, you can go for the same retailer's **Château Le Cazal Minervois** (around £4.99). This thrilling **16.5 point** red offers the sort of texture M & S would love to offer in its clothes if it could: a cross between wool and velvet. The fruit has fine berries and coagulated tannins and the overall effect is complex yet very easy to get on with.

The wine with dessert? Simple. Ask one of the guests to buy and bring along **M & S's** sublime **Moscatel de Valencia 2001** (16.5 points, £3.99). Yes, all right, this is cheating on a massive scale, but then what about Silvena's pesto sauce? You have to buy (or make) that and amortise the price over more than one recipe, don't you? They said writing the column, let alone compiling this book, would be biting off more than I could chew, but I said if Silvena's doing the cooking I'll happily chew anything.

JERUSALEM ARTICHOKE SOUP with CARAMELISED CHESTNUTS

A Jerusalem artichoke is a small root vegetable, in no way related to the green hard-leafed globe artichoke with which we are familiar. It is perfect for soups or added to potato mash, much in the same way as we use celeriac. It has a creamy, milky and slightly starchy consistency, and has rather a short season. The recipe below features one other very wintry ingredient, chestnuts. Added to the Jerusalem artichokes, these lend a certain elegance and finesse to the soup.

    300g Jerusalem artichokes
    1 onion, sliced
    5 tbsp melted butter
    800ml vegetable stock (see page 197)
    12 fresh chestnuts, cooked (see overleaf), peeled and chopped
    1 garlic clove, halved
    2 tbsp lemon juice
    salt and pepper
    4 tbsp double cream

Peel the Jerusalem artichokes, cut into pieces and wash them. Place with the onion and half of the butter in a heavy pan, and sauté for about 5 minutes. Add the stock, bring to the boil, then simmer for 20 minutes.

Meanwhile, place the rest of the butter in a small pan and add the chestnuts, garlic and lemon juice. Cook gently until almost caramelised, then season. Discard the garlic halves.

When the soup is cooked, purée in a food processor, and stir in the cream. Serve the soup garnished with the caramelised chestnuts.

COST £2.10

LAMB cooked with CHESTNUTS and POMEGRANATES

A delicious, exotic and warming lamb stew, with a very exciting mix of ingredients. It has a slight Persian influence but it actually originates from Azerbaijan, where the cuisine exhibits an ingenious combination of flavours and is known for its use of subtle aromatic herbs. The flavour particular to this stew is imparted by chestnuts and sweet pomegranates.

400g fresh chestnuts
4 tbsp vegetable oil
2 onions, chopped
1/4 tsp ground turmeric
600g boneless leg of lamb, cut into 2cm pieces
1/4 tsp ground cinnamon
1/4 tsp saffron threads
5 tbsp chopped mint
100g shelled walnuts, halved
200ml pomegranate juice
2 tbsp tomato paste
300ml chicken stock (see page 197)
3 tbsp lemon juice
salt and pepper

Preheat the oven to 200°C/400°F/Gas 6.

Cut a cross on the shell of each of the chestnuts. Place them on a baking tray and roast in the preheated oven for 30 minutes. Peel the shells and skins off when they are cool.

Heat the oil in a heavy saucepan and sauté the onion for a few minutes, then add the turmeric and lamb and cook until the meat is browned, about 10–15 minutes.

Add the cinnamon, saffron, most of the mint, the walnuts, pomegranate juice and tomato paste. Mix well and finally add the stock. Cover and simmer on a low heat for about 1¹/2 hours.

When the meat is tender, add the cooked chestnuts and lemon juice and season to taste. Simmer for 10 more minutes, then garnish with the remaining mint and serve.

COST £10.30

PANETTONE BREAD and BUTTER PUDDING with
GOLDEN SULTANAS SOAKED in AGED BALSAMIC VINEGAR

If I were to have a restaurant, this would have to be my signature dish. Using any leftovers of panettone you may have after Christmas, it is the best bread and butter pudding recipe you will ever find, and the most luxurious! I cook it in a bain-marie, which allows the pudding to remain very moist and creamy. Get the best-quality sultanas, semi-dry, and soak them overnight in the best-quality aged balsamic vinegar. Words do not do justice in describing the taste!

150g plump golden sultanas
50ml aged balsamic vinegar
200g unsalted butter, melted
500g panettone, sliced in small triangular pieces
6 eggs
40g caster sugar
300ml milk
300ml double cream

Soak the sultanas in the balsamic vinegar overnight.

Preheat the oven to 140°C/275°F/Gas 1, and grease a 25cm square dish with a little of the butter. Arrange the panettone pieces in the dish and pour over it the remaining melted butter.

Whisk the eggs and sugar until thick and creamy. Boil the milk and cream together and pour it into the egg mixture. Mix well and slowly pour over the panettone. Sprinkle with the soaked sultanas.

Cover the dish with foil and place in a large deep tray, filled with hot water. Place in the preheated oven and cook for an hour.

When ready, take out of the oven, remove the foil and, if you wish, you can sprinkle with some extra sugar and brown under the grill. Serve hot or cold.

COST £7.50

THE WINE SELECTION

Heavens to Murgatroyd! What an incredibly luxurious set of dishes, my dear Silvena. I am hugely tempted to stray from the path of the straight and narrow, budget-wise, and say to the hell with it but that is not, upon sober reflection, my brief. However, there is nothing to disbar me from sliding in, tossing out as it were, a few extravagant suggestions is there?

That Jerusalem artichoke soup with caramelised chestnuts (imagine the sight and sound of it on a menu in Lyons – *potage de topinambours aux marrons caramelisés!*) doubtless inspires you with thoughts of an ancient smelly **Pinot Noir**, but though this sounds perfect, do not forget the richness of those chestnuts and their alchemical transformation into something exotic via caramelisation. Therefore, a slightly more rugged red is required (and one which could carry on through to the next course). My suggestion is **Asda's** non-vintage **Argentinian Red (15.5 points, £2.52)** which seems to start very dry but soon the rich cherry and raspberry fruit puts in an appearance and it lingers, though not altogether lushly, and the tannins appear and a smile spreads across the drinker's face. A couple of bottles of this wine will see you through the soup and out the other side of the next which is the lamb with more chestnuts and

that very attractive addition of pomegranates – a Persian touch indeed. Which prompts the thought, not entirely frivolous, that a **Shiraz** would be highly in keeping here and certainly one such, from **McLaren Vale** in South Australia would be a treat with the dish, and most witty it would be too (since Shiraz is an Iranian metropolis), but my budget, alas, does not permit it. You would pay around £8–10 for the right bottle (which blows my whole budget my life!) and the names to look out for are **Leasingham**, **D'Arenberg**, **Coriole**, **Wirra Wirra** and several others. Certainly these wines have more heft than the Argentine red, for they are more complex wines (though the pomegranate, mint, turmeric and cinnamon are tricky hurdles for any wine to leap and great levellers of vinous liquids).

There is another, more hedonistic, reason for spending less on the red for the first two courses, and this is that one should save something for that utterly splendid pudding. I can testify to the to-die-for qualities of this dessert and when I last had it I opened my last, and very dusty, bottle of 1983 Château d'Yquem Sauternes. If your butler can lay a hand on a bottle in your cellar, all well and good, but if not may I suggest, well within our budget, **Orange Grove Moscatel de Valencia 2002 (16.5 points, £3.79, Safeway)** from Spain in the highly decorated, screwcapped bottle which, empty, makes an excellent base for a lamp or vinaigrette mixer and pourer (with a suitable top). The fruit, more relevantly, makes an outstanding base from which to launch the last course. The wine has a wonderful honied richness with a hint of marmalade and a touch of orange peel. There are many much more expensive dessert wines which would struggle with its adornments – especially that brilliant touch of sultanas soaked in balsamic vinegar.

PS, does anyone know why Murgatroyd is so honoured? Who was he? What he did he do to achieve this expressive notoriety?

SEARED SCALLOPS with PURÉED CAULIFLOWER

Scallops are pure culinary luxury, and the unique combination of flavours here only intensifies that feeling of luxury....The cost of this dish alone takes most of my budget, but it's worth it! Scallops still in their shells are the best to get, and look for those that are diver caught. Ask your fishmonger to shell and clean them for you. The orange part of the scallop – the roe – is delicious to eat, but some chefs like to remove it. It is a personal choice.

12 scallops, cleaned
knob of butter
olive oil
sea salt

Cauliflower purée
300g cauliflower florets
200ml milk
4 tbsp double cream
salt and pepper

To make the cauliflower purée, place the cauliflower florets in a saucepan and cover with the milk. Let it just come to the boil and then simmer until the florets are soft. Drain immediately and liquidise, adding the cream and seasoning. The cauliflower purée is now ready. It should have a very thick consistency. Keep warm.

To cook the scallops, place some butter with a drop of olive oil in a heavy pan. When hot, add the scallops four at a time to flash-fry, about a minute or two on each side. Scallops need very little cooking, and if over-cooked they will become tough.

To assemble, spoon three small pools of the cauliflower purée about 2cm from each other on a plate, and place a scallop on the top of each of them. Serve immediately.

COST £13.20

POLENTA with CAVOLO NERO and GORGONZOLA DOLCE CREAM SAUCE

This polenta dish is 'out of this world'. I was blown away by it when I had it in a famous Italian restaurant in London. Since then, while cooking at Books for Cooks in the past few years, I have regularly been asked to prepare it for the enjoyment of foodies, like Malcolm, who visit the shop. Cavolo nero is an Italian vegetable not dissimilar to spinach in colour (although darker green) and to cabbage in texture. The flavour is stronger than both!

450g fresh cavolo nero, washed and cut into small pieces
olive oil
2 garlic cloves, finely sliced
100g dry instant polenta
350ml water or vegetable stock (see page 197)
knob of butter
salt and pepper
25g Parmesan shavings
Gorgonzola dolce cream sauce
100g Gorgonzola dolce cheese, crumbled
50ml double cream

To prepare the Gorgonzola dolce sauce, warm the cheese in a small saucepan until melted, but do not boil. Add the cream and keep warm.

Blanch the cavolo nero in some boiling water until soft, and drain well. Heat a little olive oil in a large saucepan and fry the garlic to just soften. Add the cavolo nero and cook for about 3 minutes. Drain and purée the cavolo nero and garlic, and keep warm.

To cook the polenta, bring the water or stock to boiling point. Add the polenta all at once and reduce the heat to low, stirring constantly. The polenta will thicken while cooking. Because we are using instant polenta the cooking process is very quick, about 3–4 minutes. (The consistency should be pourable. If it's too thin, add some more hot water.) Add the butter and season well.

While the polenta is still hot, stir in the cavolo nero purée and serve immediately on individual plates. Drizzle some Gorgonzola dolce sauce over the polenta, then add some Parmesan shavings just before offering the plate.

Cost £3.60

LIME CHEESECAKE with ALMOND CRUST

This is the 'queen' of cheesecakes, and I think there is nothing like it. Limes work beautifully with crushed almonds, and once eaten, never forgotten! When I used to work at Books for Cooks in London, this was amongst the most requested and favourite desserts. This cake will serve eight to ten people.

Crust
5 tbsp melted butter
200g ground almonds
4 tbsp caster sugar

Filling
800g cream cheese
350g caster sugar
4 eggs, beaten
8 tbsp lime juice

Preheat the oven to 180°C/350°F/Gas 4. Use 1 tbsp of the melted butter for the crust to grease a 24cm springform cake tin.

For the crust, mix together the almonds, remaining melted butter and sugar and press gently into the bottom of the greased cake tin. Chill for 30 minutes.

Put the cream cheese and sugar in a bowl of an electric mixer and beat at low speed until the mixture is very smooth. Add the eggs and mix well. Finally add the lime juice.

Pour the filling into the cake tin and set on a baking sheet. Bake for about 45 minutes, until the cheesecake is set. It should still be slightly wobbly in the middle, though. Allow to cool, then chill before serving.

COST £3.60

THE WINE SELECTION

This menu is so absurdly and outrageously sybaritic that it calls for a vastly greater talent than my own. I am a mere ten-quid tippler. I am not up to finding a wine suitable for such a luxurious repast. Scallops with creamed cauliflower? The wine to so effortlessly accompany this dish is a satin-textured Alsatian Tokay-Pinot Gris, something bearing the Zind-Humbrecht label, but my resources do not stretch that far. All I can offer is **Somerfield's Hilltop Riverview Pinot Gris 2001 (14 points, under £3.99)** from Hungary with its appealing spicy edge. As for the polenta with its Gorgonzola sauce, all I can do is throw my hands up in despair. I happen to know for a fact that Britain's greatest French chef has eaten this dish, cooked for him by Silvena, and he remarked that it was the most marvellous polenta he had ever eaten. What did he drink with it? Not **Somerfield's** own-label **Argentine Sangiovese 2001 (16 points, under a fiver** last time I looked). This is a pity for it would be marvellous with the dish, for the wine has a firm edge of black cherries and blackberries and it is best – please, trust me – served lightly chilled. It is, I suppose, difficult not also to suggest an Italian wine with this dish and my choice would be a Barolo, but the one I'd like to suggest is, as far as I am aware, only available at the Edinburgh wine merchants **Valvona & Crolla**. It is **Barbaresco San Lorenzo Angelo Gaja 1982 (20 points)**. It's a snip at £220. I last drank a bottle of the wine some four or five years ago and it was an experience I will never forget. It has licorice and tannins to die for. I should warn you, if it is not obvious, that the wine might, indeed will, have changed since I last tasted it and 20 points might now be an exaggeration of monumental proportions. Well, we can all dream, can't we?

Lastly and most agonisingly, I have to face that utterly to-die-for lime cheesecake with its almond crust. It has to have an unctuous dessert wine but where do I find the money? Oh to hell with it. The wine has to be **Matusalem Dulce Muy Viejo Oloroso (18 points, £10.99** the half bottle, **Waitrose)**. Yes, madam, it is a sherry. It is one of the world's most stunning sweet wines (ambrosial, balsam-like texturally). Yes, I know it's more than I can afford. But what can I do? Blame the chef. She's the one over the top.

CRISP AUBERGINE, FETA and CARAMELISED SHALLOT SALAD

A wonderful and very light starter. It can be prepared earlier, and assembled at the last minute just before serving. I love to serve this salad with sheeps' feta cheese but goats' cheese also goes very well with it.

    1 medium aubergine, washed
    6 tbsp olive oil
    3 shallots, thinly sliced
    200g fresh rocket leaves
    2 tbsp balsamic vinegar
    salt and pepper
    100g sheeps' feta cheese, crumbled
    2 tbsp mint leaves

Thinly slice the aubergine. Brush each slice with oil, using about 4 tbsp. Place a heavy non-stick frying pan over a medium high heat and when hot cook the aubergine slices for about 2 minutes on each side, a few at a time, until golden and crisp. Keep aside.

To cook the shallots, heat the remaining olive oil in another frying pan. Add the shallots and cook slowly to caramelise them. This will take about 6–8 minutes over a medium heat.

Toss the rocket with the balsamic vinegar, seasoning to taste, and divide between four serving plates. Place some crisp aubergine on top of each, then some crumbled feta, finishing with the caramelised shallots and some mint leaves.

COST £3.80

BRAISED DUCK with ALMOND and POMEGRANATE SAUCE

From Azerbaijan, a delicious stew, which has slight Persian flavours. The sauce is particularly delicious, and the dish is best served with a rice pilaff. Pomegranates are still around at this time, and you will need their juice for this recipe. The combination of almonds and pomegranates is very exotic and exciting, but subtle to western tastes.

1 large duck, about 2kg
2 tsp olive oil
1 large Spanish onion, chopped
½ tsp ground turmeric
250ml chicken stock (see page 197)
300g ground almonds
500ml fresh pomegranate juice, about 5–6 large pomegranates, or
   bottled juice
4 tbsp lemon juice
1 tsp caster sugar
½ tsp ground cardamom
salt and pepper

First of all prepare the duck. Quarter it, rinse well and dry thoroughly with paper towels.

Heat the oil in a large non-stick casserole, and brown the duck pieces on all sides, a few at a time. Remove the duck and keep warm.

Now add the onion to the casserole, and sauté for few minutes in the duck fat, stirring over a medium heat. Add the turmeric and cook for a further 5 minutes. Add the chicken stock and bring to the boil. Turn down to a simmer, then add the almonds and pomegranate juice, and continue simmering for another 20 minutes. Stir in the lemon juice, sugar and cardamom, and season to taste.

Now return the duck quarters to the casserole, cover, and cook on a medium heat for at least 1½ hours or until the duck is cooked. Serve hot.

COST £12.60

CHESTNUT, MAPLE SYRUP and BAILEY'S CUSTARD with TOASTED MACADAMIAS

Everybody knows that chestnut and chocolate make a perfect combination, but here is another no less impressive partnership, chestnut and maple syrup. The custard combines the tremendous flavours of the maple and chestnuts and is finished with the essential crunch of the slightly toasted macadamia nuts. It's an unpredictably delicious winter dessert.

150g raw chestnuts, cooked as on page 76
150ml maple syrup
350ml double cream
3 egg yolks
1 egg
4 tbsp Bailey's Irish Cream
60 shelled macadamia nuts, chopped and toasted

Preheat the oven to 180°C/350°F/Gas 4.

When you are able to handle the chestnuts, remove their skins and chop them roughly.

Simmer the maple syrup and chestnuts together for 30 minutes until the liquid is slightly reduced.

In a food processor purée the maple syrup and chestnuts, double cream, egg yolks, egg and Bailey's until smooth. Place in a shallow, ovenproof glass dish, and bake in a water bath (a roasting tray with enough hot water to come halfway up the sides of the dish) for 25 minutes. Cool and refrigerate.

To serve, garnish with toasted macadamias.

COST £3.20

THE WINE SELECTION

Feta and caramelised shallots? Rocket leaves? Balsamic vinegar? Mint? Tip-toe with feather-light feet around this starter. It can sting you. As it will sting the palate (deliciously, Silvena, deliciously*). How, though, to find a wine to accompany it which will not likewise sting the pocket? I recommend **Tesco's** own-label **Chilean Sauvignon Blanc (16 points, £3.47)** which parades ripe gooseberry with citrus and has the weight of fruit and the acidic balance to just about grin and bear those ingredients without wincing. A single bottle should see the four of you through that first course, the palate stung deliciously, the pocket unstung delightfully.

Now with that braised duck with its amazing almond and pomegranate sauce – 'which has slight Persian flavours' says Silvena but there's nothing slight about anything connected with that gal – I am tempted to be witty and suggest, as I did with another menu (which also had a Persian side to it), that a Shiraz would be highly in keeping here. Shiraz is an Iranian, a Persian city, and they grow vines there, too, though whether they still make wine I doubt. The nearest we get nowadays to a wine on a UK shelf with Iran in the name is Irancy, a red wine from Auxerre in lower Burgundy. Such a wine would be hopeless with that chicken. But not an Aussie Shiraz; indeed not. But is there one within my budget? Nope. However, the Grenache grape can come to our rescue, and with **Majestic's 16 points Grange du Midi Grenache 2002 (£3.99)** we acquire a big, richly, tenaciously berried red, broad-bottomed and dry. And we need a broad bottom to our wine. Of course, if money is no object then an abundance of exuberant Aussie reds suggest themselves but one in

---

* Bulgarian cooks are extremely sensitive to unjust remarks or misunderstood comments, whereas British chefs are so used to having rudeness and criticism – and sometimes their own creations – flung in their faces that they are inured.

particular strikes me as perfect and it is not a Shiraz. It is
**Knappstein Enterprise Cabernet Sauvignon 1999 (16.5 points,
Oddbins, under £10)**. It is deliciously mature and curiously so in that
it seems to me to unite elements of California and northern Italy in
its make-up. This is to compliment the wine for we get lithe tannins,
sweet black cherry and roasted plum fruit with a sweetness
containing a hint of licorice.

With that crazy pud – chestnuts, toasted macadamia nuts, maple
syrup and Bailey's custard? – we cannot stay within sensible
budgetary grounds. This stunning dessert takes us into the world of
truly rich, honied white wines where the words ambrosial, luscious,
nectareous, mellifluous (or should that be melliferous?), luxurious,
honied, sybaritic and hedonistic spring effortlessly to mind.
Unctuous and raunchily sweet, at **Safeway**, is **Nederburg Noble Late
Harvest 2002** from the Cape. This rates **16.5 points** for its thick
honied fruit with hints of spice, citrus and pineapple. It costs £5.99
in the half bottle and it will happily live alongside that tongue-
tangling pudding. Let us hope Morrisons, who now own Safeway,
keep stocking this wine.

SALAD of ASPARAGUS on BEETROOT CARPACCIO with BALSAMIC CREAM

Asparagus is wonderfully crisp on the outside and tender on the inside and I think it is truly elevated in this recipe. The balsamic cream coating it adds a richness that isn't usually associated with vinaigrette – or asparagus, for that matter.

300g asparagus stalks, cut into 2.5cm lengths
salt and pepper
2 medium beetroots, boiled and skinned, then very finely sliced
100g frisée (tender leaves only), or any small leaf salad
olive oil

Balsamic cream
100g double cream
1 tsp balsamic vinegar

Blanch the asparagus in boiling salted water until just cooked, then chill in iced water. Drain and dry on paper towels.

For the balsamic cream, whisk the cream in a bowl and just as it thickens slightly, fold in the balsamic vinegar and some salt and pepper to taste.

To serve, place a 7.5cm ring mould on to the middle of a plate and place a quarter of the slices of beetroot in it in a fan-like fashion, slightly overlapping. Gently lift off the mould and repeat with the remaining three plates.

Toss the asparagus in just enough cream mixture to coat. Stack about a quarter of the asparagus on to the middle of the beetroot carpaccio, leaving about a 1cm border of beetroot.

Toss the frisée with a drizzle of olive oil. For each plate take about a handful of frisée, twist it in the palm of your hand to make a small bundle, and set it gently on the stack of asparagus.

COST £4.45

CITRUS SALMON with ORANGE CONFIT

Salmon has become a rather 'common' fish. Years ago it was very pricy and a treat on our tables, but today, because it is now farmed in large quantities, salmon is very reasonably priced and has become a lot more familiar. We seem to have run out of exciting ways to cook it, though, so here is a recipe that will help you rediscover how wonderful salmon is. It's a very light and zesty dish with a twist, the salmon cured and flavoured with ground citrus zest, and finished with an orange confit.

600g salmon fillet, skin and pin bones removed
handful of chives, finely chopped

Citrus marinade
finely grated zest of ¹/₂ lemon
finely grated zest of 1 orange
finely grated zest of ¹/₂ lime
finely grated zest of ¹/₂ grapefruit
1 tbsp sea salt
1 tbsp caster sugar
¹/₂ tbsp ground white pepper

Orange confit
2 medium oranges
100ml sugar syrup (see page 200)
¹/₄ tsp white wine vinegar

For the marinade, combine all the ingredients in a bowl.

Cut a piece of foil, slightly longer than the salmon fillet, and place the salmon on it. Coat the salmon with the zesty marinade. Bring the sides of the foil together over the top of the fish and roll the foil down to form a packet. Marinate the fillet for about 3 hours. If you leave it for any longer, the fish will be over-salted.

To make the orange confit, using a sharp knife, remove the peel and slice between the membranes to remove all the orange segments. Boil the sugar syrup and add the white wine vinegar. Pour over the orange segments and leave to cool.

Remove the fish from the foil and rinse off the marinade. Dry the fillet well and cut into four portions. Place the fillets in a steamer and cook for about 6–8 minutes. To test if the salmon is cooked, remove a piece and bend it slightly: it should begin to flake. When cooked, remove the salmon and keep warm.

To serve, warm the orange segments gently through in the syrup and place about four next to each other, side by side to form a rectangle in the centre of the plate. Place a fillet over the orange confit, and sprinkle with some chives.

COST £7.80

WHITE CHOCOLATE and VANILLA MOUSSE

White chocolate and vanilla are beautifully suited, a marriage suggested by my nine-year-old son, Alex. For years I prepared this mousse *without* the vanilla, and it was only last year that I discovered how delicious it is *with*. This recipe will serve about eight portions.

200g crème pâtissière (see page 201), warm
300g white chocolate, broken into pieces
2 vanilla pods, split and seeds scraped
600ml double cream, semi-whipped

First make the crème pâtissière using any basic recipe (or see page 201).

Melt the chocolate in a bowl over a pan of boiling water (the bowl must not touch the water). Once melted, add the scraped vanilla seeds and mix well. Now add the crème pâtissière and leave to cool.

Fold the whipped cream into the cold mixture and pour it into a tray that is about 20 x 10cm and at least 2.5cm deep. Leave to set overnight.

To serve, spoon two small quenelles, or oval scoops, into each dessert plate. You can also spoon into individual serving glasses and leave to set.

COST £6.87

THE WINE SELECTION

You just can't trust cooks, can you? Just when I thought finding the right wines for the money was going so swimmingly, along comes another impossible menu. Silvena, my dear Silvena...how can I put this? Your ideas are just too...well, just too impossibly challenging. That salad of baby asparagus to start is about as easy to find a partner for as a stone-deaf tango dancer with a wooden leg. It screams out for a New Zealand Sauvignon Blanc but that's seven or eight quid blown right away. The only wine which might work and is within budget is **Waitrose's Riverview Sauvignon Blanc 2001 (16 points, £3.99)** from Hungary. It has an appealing, chewy, gooseberry richness. For the marinated salmon with its lethal orange confit, I would go for an Alsatian Gewürztraminer but it's too pricey and so, rather craftily I must admit, I am going to chill a bottle of red wine: **Les Nivières Saumur 2001 (16.5 points, £3.69, Waitrose)**. This is dry but has a raspberry tang and a hint of slate on the finish. Will it survive that citrus confit? You might as well ask me if I know the dead cert winner of the 3.15 at Kempton Park. I can only make an educated guess. I would in fact go for many young Loire reds, from the silky Cabernet Franc grape, from Chinon or Bourgueil or Saumur Champigny and chill it with this dish.

And now comes the course you thought impossible: white chocolate mousse. Since you're in **Waitrose** you may as well carry on the way you've started, and so you spend just £3.99 on a **16-point** half bottle of **Maury Vin Doux Naturel** which is a fortified red (16.5% alcohol) from Catalan France. It knows a few things about chocolate, this sweet red wine, and who ever thought you'd find the relevant bottle so cheaply? Failing to find this specimen, I suggest a sweetie from Spain at **Majestic: Pedro Ximénez Viejo Napoleon Hidalgo (18 points, £8.99)**. It offers toffee apple and crème brûlée with chocolate molasses and butterscotch, with an oily honied toffee on the finish.

CANNELLINI BEANS with SAUTÉED MUSHROOMS and THYME

Dried beans are not all the same. It is important to get beans that are no more than a year or two old, preferably the harvest of the year before. You will find that a lot of dried pulses sold out there are much older. Tell-tale signs are wrinkled skins and discoloration, so try and get yours from a reputable supplier. Here, deliciously velvet-textured cannellini beans are paired with sautéed field mushrooms – the most scrumptious of winter foods.

300g dried cannellini beans, soaked overnight
juice of 1 lemon
4 tbsp single cream
salt and pepper
olive oil
250g field mushrooms, wiped and sliced
4 garlic cloves, crushed
handful of thyme leaves

Drain the beans after their overnight soak, then cook them in boiling water until tender, about 45–60 minutes. Drain and purée. Add the lemon juice and single cream. Mix well and season to taste.

Heat 2 tbsp oil in a frying pan, add the sliced mushrooms, and sauté with the garlic until browned. Finally add most of the thyme leaves.

Serve the bean purée topped with sautéed mushrooms. Drizzle with some more olive oil, and sprinkle with the remaining thyme.

COST £3.50

ORANGE and MUSTARD MARINATED PORK
with ORANGE and ROCKET SALAD

When cooking with pork it is very important to get really good-quality meat or you risk never wanting to cook pork again! Pork is at its best in the winter. Try to buy outdoor-reared pork, because it has so much more flavour than the commercially produced one. Orange is a wonderful companion to pork, its acidity giving a perfect balance. Use the zest in the marinade, and the segments in the salad.

4 pork cutlets, about 200g each
400g baby potatoes, scrubbed and boiled
knob of butter

Marinade
finely grated zest of 2 oranges (see below)
150ml orange juice
1 tbsp English mustard
3 tsp soy sauce
1 tbsp white wine vinegar
1 tbsp brown sugar

Orange and rocket salad
2 oranges, segmented (zest them first)
1 avocado, peeled, stoned and sliced
200g rocket leaves, washed and dried
200g green beans, blanched in boiling water for few minutes
1 tbsp white wine vinegar
salt and pepper

For the marinade combine all the ingredients in a bowl and whisk well. Place the pork cutlets in a glass or ceramic dish and pour half of the marinade over it. Cover and refrigerate for at least 6 hours or preferably overnight.

Bring the pork back to room temperature, then drain off and discard the marinade. Cook the cutlets on a hotplate or hot frying pan, or grill under a well preheated grill, until tender, about 8–10 minutes on each side.

Meanwhile, make the salad. Combine all the ingredients, except for the vinegar, in a bowl. Whisk the vinegar into the remaining half of the marinade and season to taste. Pour the mixture over the salad and toss.

Serve the pork cutlets with the salad and hot baby potatoes tossed in butter.

COST £12.50

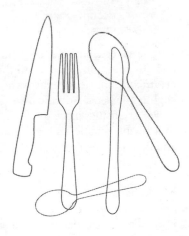

BANANA FRITTERS with PALM SUGAR and COCONUT CREAM SAUCE

My husband tells me that his mother used to make apple and banana fritters when he was young, and though I love my mother-in-law dearly, they surely could not have been as mouth-watering as these. The batter is particularly light and fluffy and when cooked the fritters are crispy on the outside and meltingly soft on the inside.

Palm sugar comes in both light and dark varieties, and is sold in just about every Asian shop as well as some supermarkets. It is usually in solid chunks and you can grate off what you need. It has a wonderfully distinctive caramel/maple flavour.

4 bananas, peeled and halved
vegetable oil for deep-frying

Batter
100g plain flour
a pinch of salt
2 tbsp melted butter
2 egg whites

Palm sugar and coconut cream sauce
100g palm sugar, grated
200ml coconut cream
juice of 1 lime

For the sauce, combine the palm sugar and 2 tbsp water in a saucepan and stir over a low heat until the sugar dissolves. Stir in the coconut cream and simmer over a low heat for 5–10 minutes or until the cream slightly thickens. Add the lime juice and stir to combine.

For the batter, place the flour in a bowl with a pinch of salt, make a well in the middle and add about 150ml water. Whisk until smooth and then add the melted butter. Whisk the egg whites until firm peaks form, then carefully fold into the batter mixture in two batches.

Heat the oil in a pan or deep-fat fryer to 180°C/350°F. Dip the halved bananas into the batter, tap off any excess, and deep-fry in the hot oil for about 2–3 minutes or until golden. Drain and serve immediately, drizzled with the palm sugar and coconut cream sauce.

COST £3.80

THE WINE SELECTION

There is, in this menu, the first leaning towards rusticity that our
elegant and flavoursome chef has shown in her approach to creating
her dishes. That is not a condemnation. On the contrary. It is delight.
I am jumping around the cellar with it. That starter of cannellini
beans with sautéed mushrooms, with pork and arugula salad to
follow makes my life supremely easy (which is the essence of the
rustic, as opposed to the agricultural, existence, is it not?). A wine
which will cope with the sensitive harmony of flavours in the first
course without overwhelming them but then be bold enough to
combat that potent marinated meat has got to have a peasant edge to
it. We cannot be having a delicate Burgundy for example or an
outrageously austere Bordeaux – in any case such wines are remote
from my budget. An Aussie Shiraz perhaps (Tesco and Sainsbury's
own-labels are excellent under a fiver)? A South African Pinotage
(Sainsbury's own-label is excellent)? A Californian Zinfandel (one of
the Bonterra organic range from Fetzer would be good)? We are
getting warmer here, but not much cheaper. Money no object, I
suggest we go for a **Knappstein Cabernet Sauvignon** from the Clare
Valley (£15 or so from **Oddbins**) or one of those lush but elegant
Margaret River, Western Australian Cabernets like Cullen.

The bottle to mix it successfully with banana fritters? I can only
suggest the acquisition of a half bottle of **Majestic's** extraordinary
Elysium Black Muscat 2001 (17 points, around £7), made by Andrew
Quady in sunny California. Later vintages will be every bit as good
with a wine like this, and so you can pour it with this sumptuous
dessert with confidence (some hedonists might pour it over this pud
as well but this would severely disrupt Silvena's ideas and we can't
have that).

SPRING

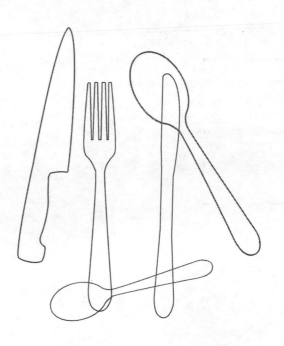

SWEET POTATO SOUP with CORIANDER PESTO

A smooth, velvety-textured sweet potato soup with a dollop of crunchy coriander pesto! Use reddy-brown skinned sweet potatoes as they have bright orange flesh and a sweet creamy flavour. The pesto here is made with coriander instead of basil, and has a different character as I have added chilli. All those ingredients work very well together to create a slightly exotic experience.

1 onion, finely chopped
3 garlic cloves, chopped
2 tbsp olive oil
400g sweet potatoes, peeled and diced
650ml hot vegetable stock (see page 197) or water
salt and pepper
Tabasco sauce

Pesto
small bunch of coriander
45g pine nuts
3 garlic cloves
1 fresh green chilli, seeded
100ml olive oil

For the pesto, place everything except the oil in a food processor and blend to a coarse purée. Add the oil slowly with the motor running, using as much as you think to make your pesto the way you like it. I like my pesto of a rather thick consistency.

For the soup, sauté the onion and garlic in the oil until softened, then add the potatoes. Almost immediately add about 100ml of the hot stock and let it simmer for about 10 minutes. Add the remaining stock and cook until the potato is very soft, another 25 minutes.

Now place the soup in a food processor to purée. Return the smooth, creamy soup to the pan and season to taste, adding a dash of Tabasco. Serve while hot, spooning a dollop of coriander-chilli pesto on to each helping.

COST £4.15

HONEY, CORIANDER and FENNEL GLAZED CHICKEN with SALSIFY PURÉE

The mild flavour and slightly dense texture of chicken are perfectly suited to the delicate aromatic combination of coriander and fennel. It makes a surprising and elegant combination with the silky textured, sweet-bitter salsify purée. Salsify is a root vegetable with a rather unique flavour and in my recipe I am using 'black' salsify – known as scorzonera – with a strong, slightly bitter flavour and tender flesh. The salsify plant was formerly used in Spain to treat snake bites, it's so good for you....Salsify is in season in spring, and is best available from farmers' markets around the country.

80ml clear honey
4 tsp coriander seeds, coarsely ground
4 tsp fennel seeds
2 tbsp grated fresh root ginger
4 chicken breasts, boned with skin on
salt and pepper

Salsify purée
500g salsify
200ml water
200ml milk
50g butter

To make the salsify purée, prepare the salsify for cooking first of all. Salsify looks like black, long wooden sticks, and has a moist and creamy interior. Scrape and peel the salsify roots with a potato peeler, then cut into chunks, wash and put them straight into a bowl containing the water and milk, which will avoid discoloration. When ready to cook, transfer to a saucepan with the milk-water mixture and bring to the boil, adding some salt to taste. Cook until soft, about 20–25 minutes. Drain, and purée the salsify in a food processor. Add the butter.

For the chicken, first make the glaze by combining the honey, coriander, fennel and ginger. Season the chicken with salt and pepper and place skin down in a very hot sauté pan to brown for about 2–3 minutes. Turn over and brush with the glaze. Reduce the heat to medium and cook for about 10 minutes or until done. Brush with the remaining glaze and keep warm.

To serve, spoon some salsify purée into the centre of each plate. Place a sliced chicken breast over the top.

COST £9.90

GOAT'S CHEESECAKE

A special treat for lovers of sweet-savoury tastes! This recipe will serve about eight people. The soft-textured goat's cheese is a wonderful base for any citrus fruits – for instance, limes will work very well too.

    butter for greasing
    300g goat's cheese
    125g caster sugar
    2 tsp vanilla extract
    3 tbsp finely grated lemon zest
    3 tbsp lemon juice
    6 eggs, separated
    2 tbsp plain flour

Preheat the oven to 180°C/350°F/Gas 4, and butter a 16cm round tin.

In a bowl, combine the cheese, sugar, vanilla, lemon zest and juice, then mix with a hand-held mixer, adding the egg yolks one by one. Stir in the flour. Whip the egg whites until soft peaks form, then gently fold them in the cheese mixture, making sure you do not over-mix.

Spread the mixture into the prepared tin. Bake the cheesecake for about 30 minutes or until cooked. Let it cool completely before serving.

Serve with fresh fruits if desired.

COST £4.60

THE WINE SELECTION

I am tickled to report that, thanks to J. Sainsbury plc, this menu is about
to enjoy its most complete moment. This is because not only are we able
to afford an aperitif but two bottles of red to go with the main course and
a dessert wine to go with the pud. The meal will commence, or rather the
pre-dinner drinks will commence, with a single bottle of **Sainsbury's** own-
label **Vermouth Rosso (17 points, £2.99)** which is a superb cross, though
blatant copy might be a better term, between Campari and Martini. That
absurd price is partly made possible by only 14.7% of alcohol whereas the
big-name brands are stronger. The Sainsbury's product is deliciously
bitter and sweet and so we will chill the bottle thoroughly and hand out
four glasses of it, no ice, absolutely no ice, each glass garnished with a
thin slice of orange and lemon. This will induce a lovely mood for the
first course of sweet potato soup which is unaccompanied by any wine
(though you can serve the red if you like) until we reach the glazed
chicken breast and salsify purée. Here again **Sainsbury's** comes to our
rescue for the wine we are serving with it is lightly chilled **Bondi Blue
Merlot 2001 (15 points, £2.99)** from Australia. It's plummy and soft and
it'll be terrific with that chicken because its glaze is so tricky to combat.

And then we come to that gorgeous goat's cheesecake and yet again
Sainsbury's is hero because we're going to drink with it the own-label
Rich Cream Sherry (16.5 points, £3.99) with its crème-brûlée-rich fruit.
What a feast! And all for a tenner! Well, just a bit over a tenner...£2.96
over to be precise. Hedonism on a budget isn't always a piece of cake. Of
course, that Bondi Merlot will be a different vintage when this book
appears and so since I'm suspicious that the follow-on vintage will not be
as good, I'm going to have to suggest something else for that robust
chicken. It is **Kir Yianni Imathia Syrah (16 points, £9.99, Oddbins)** from
Greece. The 2000 vintage of this wine was aged in new French oak for 12
months and spent six months in bottle before release and the result was a
nicely mature yet sprightly specimen. It was very dry and earthy yet
vivaciously fruity. It has a most curious, and curiously delicious,
undertone of burned, creamy berries with a hint of dried fig and it is this
aspect of the wine which commends it to me with that chicken. I daresay
later vintages of this wine will perform similarly but I cannot guarantee it.

LENTIL and APRICOT SOUP
BULGARIAN LAMB with PRUNES
POACHED PLUMS with ROSEWATER SORBET

LENTIL and APRICOT SOUP

It's time to show my true colours, for I am East European after all! This soup is from my homeland, and is a very light and elegant dish. Lentils are the most exciting of pulses: I use them not only in soups, but also for stuffing, in salads and in terrines. The dried apricots are a Middle Eastern touch and blend beautifully in colour and taste with the red lentils. It all becomes bright orange and almost luminous when cooked.

3 tbsp olive oil
1 large onion, finely chopped
3 garlic cloves, finely chopped
50g dried apricots, chopped
300g dried split red lentils
1 litre vegetable stock (see page 197) or water
3 medium tomatoes, peeled and chopped, or use canned tomatoes
1/2 tsp ground cumin
handful of thyme leaves
juice of 1 lemon
salt and pepper
handful of flat-leaf parsley, chopped

Heat the oil in a large heavy saucepan on a medium heat. Add the onion, garlic and dried apricots. Sauté, stirring, until the onions are soft, about 10 minutes. Add the lentils and stock and bring to the boil. Reduce the heat and simmer, covered, until the lentils are soft and tender, about 20–30 minutes.

Add the tomatoes, cumin and thyme, and simmer for another 15 minutes.

Spoon the soup into a food processor and purée in batches. Return the purée to the saucepan and add the lemon juice, and salt and pepper to taste. Sprinkle liberally with the parsley, and serve hot.

Cost £2.80

BULGARIAN BRAISED LAMB with PRUNES

In Bulgaria dried prunes have a wonderfully smoky flavour. Dried fruit is used a lot in wintertime, when fresh seasonal fruit is not available. In this recipe I am soaking the prunes in Chinese tea (which I know is not very Bulgarian), to intensify that smoky flavour. The lamb is complemented beautifully by the subtle sweetness of the prunes. Sweet and sour tastes are very common in East European cooking.

    200ml very strong Chinese tea
    200g prunes
    5 tbsp vegetable oil
    1 large onion, finely chopped
    600g boned leg of lamb, cut into 5cm cubes (keep the bones for
        stock)
    2 tbsp plain flour
    salt and pepper
    200ml stock made from the lamb bones (see page 199)
    1 tbsp caster sugar
    5 tbsp white wine vinegar
    2 bay leaves
    1/2 tsp ground cinnamon
    pinch of ground cloves

Bring the tea to the boil and pour over the prunes. Stand for an hour. Remove the prunes, stone if necessary, and set aside.

Heat the oil in a casserole dish, add the onion and sauté until lightly coloured. Meanwhile dust the meat with flour, salt and pepper and add to the casserole. Cook until the meat is browned. Add the stock and simmer until the sauce has slightly thickened, about 20–30 minutes.

Add the sugar, vinegar, bay leaves, cinnamon, cloves and prunes. Bring to a boil, and then again simmer for about 20 more minutes until the meat is tender. Serve while hot, with either rice or boiled potatoes.

COST £ 10.90

PLUMS POACHED in ROSEWATER SYRUP
with ROSEWATER SORBET

Rosewater, a distillation of red rose petals, has the intense perfumed flavour of its source. It creates an old-fashioned rose garden in full bloom, but at the same time it has a surprisingly spicy and smoky quality. This will seem very exotic to those unfamiliar with the flavour of rosewater.

200g plums, halved and stoned
150ml sugar syrup (see page 200)
4 cloves
juice of 1 lemon
6 tbsp rosewater

Sorbet
375ml sugar syrup (see page 200)
375ml water
4 tbsp rosewater
juice of 1 lemon
1 egg white, lightly beaten

Place the plums in the sugar syrup and add the cloves and lemon juice. Simmer on a medium heat, covered, for about 10–15 minutes or until the plums are soft. Stir in the rosewater.

To make the sorbet, combine the sugar syrup, water, rosewater and lemon juice and pour into an ice-cream machine. Churn for about 5 minutes, or until it becomes opaque. Add the egg white, while still churning. Continue until the sorbet is firm enough to serve, or store in a container and place in the freezer.

To serve, place some warm poached plums on each plate with scoops of the rosewater sorbet. Spoon some syrup over.

COST £ 4.70

THE WINE SELECTION

There is always something a bit sulky about lentils. Do you know what I mean? A bit of a grudging I-could-be-haricots-verts-if-I-tried attitude. Silvena's addition of apricots to make a soup certainly puts a smile on its face but not, alas, mine. What on earth do we drink with it? The dish may well bring nostalgic tears to your eyes, my dear Bulgar, but it sounds to me like something to give to a geriatric who can't afford Viagra. In this context, as a sexy start to a meal, perhaps we need also to consider what dish follows and what do we find? More dried fruit. In Chinese tea for heaven's sake! Is this really how Bulgarian cooks carry on with lamb? I ate very well when I was last in Sofia but I don't recall so much blooming fruit (or, I must admit, such inventive culinary thinking). Well, then, there's only one answer to finding the wines to go with the first two courses of this meal. The choice must be Bulgarian red and we are spoilt for it. There are scores of sturdy Bulgarian reds on retailers' shelves, but let me pick out just three. These are **Reka Valley Bulgarian Cabernet Sauvignon (16 points, £2.79, Tesco), Bulgarian Cabernet Sauvignon, Black Sea Region 2001 (16 points, £2.99, Somerfield)**, and **Bulgarian Cabernet Sauvignon (15.5 points, £11.89** in the 3-litre box, **Sainsbury's)**. Superplonk.com lists at least a dozen others and they all rate respectably.

This leaves only the ticklish problem of what to drink with the plums poached in rosewater syrup. There is no Bulgarian wine on sale here to go with it. I suggest you drink the tea in which some of those fruits were steeped. That should be sweet enough for anyone (and if you require alcohol dash it with a slug of malt whisky). On the other hand, one wine which will suit those plums is **Nederburg Noble Late Harvest 2002** from the Cape. This rates **16.5 points** for its thick honied fruit with hints of spice, citrus and pineapple. It costs £5.99 in the half bottle at **Safeway**.

TARATOR

Tarator is classic cold yoghurt soup with cucumber. It originates from Turkey but the version here is as we serve it back home in Bulgaria. This dish is an ideal prelude to the main course with its combinations of flavours.

500ml Greek yoghurt
250ml water
salt and pepper
2 medium cucumbers, peeled, seeded and finely diced
1 small garlic clove, minced
handful of mint leaves
olive oil
40g shelled walnuts, chopped

Whisk the yoghurt with the water until smooth. Season to taste. Add the cucumber and garlic and stir well. Finally add the mint leaves and stand about 10 minutes before serving.

Serve with a drizzle of olive oil and a sprinkling of chopped walnut on top.

COST £3.50

BRAISED LAMB SHANKS with BARLEY, and EGG and LEMON SAUCE

This is a very light and healthy way of cooking lamb shanks. The usual way of preparing shanks is to braise them in rich red wine or tomato sauces. A recipe from the Caucasian mountains, the original version is cooked with saffron. The budget allows you to go for the best spring lamb, so why not indulge....Most of this dish could be prepared in advance.

olive oil
4 lamb shanks
3 shallots, finely chopped
4 garlic cloves, minced
finely grated zest of 2 lemons
small bunch of parsley, finely chopped
6 bay leaves
1.3 litres lamb stock (see page 199) or water
salt and pepper
250g pearl barley, rinsed and drained

Egg and lemon sauce
200ml cooking liquid
1 tsp cornflour
juice of 1 lemon
2 egg yolks
small bunch of coriander, finely chopped

Heat some olive oil in a heavy, deep casserole, and brown the shanks well all over, about 10 minutes. Remove and keep warm. Add the shallots to the casserole, and cook until soft, about 12 minutes. Return the lamb to the casserole. Add the garlic, lemon zest, some of the parsley, the bay leaves and 1 litre of the stock. Season to taste, bring to the boil and then simmer, covered, for about an hour.

Preheat the oven to 160°C/325°F/Gas 3.

Now add the barley and the remaining liquid and bring back to the boil. Place the casserole, still covered, in the preheated oven, and cook until the barley is done and the lamb is tender, about an hour. Once cooked, remove the shanks and keep warm. Remove and discard the bay leaves. Strain off and measure 200ml of the cooking juices and put to one side. Return the lamb to the barley, and sprinkle the dish generously with the remaining parsley.

To make the sauce, bring the reserved liquid to a simmer in a small saucepan. Add some water to the cornflour and mix into a smooth paste, adding the lemon juice and egg yolks. Add this to the simmering cooking liquid and stir well for a few minutes until cooked and thickened. Season to taste and stir in the finely chopped coriander.

Serve the lamb shanks over a small pile of barley, with some of the sauce spooned over.

Cost £13.80

RHUBARB and ELDERFLOWER JELLY

Rhubarb is just about the most exciting seasonal fruit around at this time of year. The open field crop variety is the one with most flavour. The jelly, once cooked, looks too good to eat! I am using here the juice of blood oranges to really intensify the bright colours.

450g fresh English rhubarb
100g caster sugar
5 tbsp elderflower cordial
4 gelatine leaves
juice of 2 small blood oranges

Chop the rhubarb into 2cm pieces and place in a medium saucepan. Add the sugar, elderflower cordial and about 150ml water. Simmer very gently on a very low heat until the rhubarb is very soft, about 5 minutes.

Meanwhile, soak two of the gelatine leaves briefly in cold water.

Place the hot rhubarb mixture in a food processor and blitz to a smooth purée. Place a sieve over the top of a bowl and strain the liquid out of the rhubarb mixture. All the juice will drain through and the fruit pulp remain in the sieve. Reserve the fruit pulp.

Squeeze the excess water out of the gelatine, add the gelatine to the hot rhubarb juice and mix well to dissolve. Pour the liquid into a medium oval glass dish, and leave to cool. Place in the refrigerator to set.

Meanwhile place the fruit pulp purée in a small saucepan, add the orange juice and slowly heat up. Repeat the same procedure with the remaining gelatine as above and once ready add to the hot purée. Keep aside to cool.

Once the rhubarb jelly in the fridge has set, pour over the rhubarb purée and spread evenly. Cover and leave to set. The final result is a serving of a beautifully transparent layer of pink jelly, topped with an intensely coloured and textured jelly of fruit.

COST £2.40

THE WINE SELECTION

Goodness, what a delicate menu this is, Silvena. A strapping lass like you coming up with such dainties! Perversely (or perhaps paradoxically, certainly curiously), delicate wines will disappear with it – any of it. You, gentle reader, may be seduced by the casual succulence of these dishes but do not be gulled into thinking any old wine will do. Any old wine will not do. There is to all these dishes a cunning, fresh, citrussy edge. Note the cucumber and mint with the yoghurt in the soup; the egg and lemon sauce with the lamb shanks; and the rhubarb and elderflower jelly, divine though it is, is difficult even for a seasoned dessert wine. Personally, I find liquid with liquid – soup with wine – an irritating combination (unless the soup is thick like minestrone), and my first thought, with the one in question here, is to serve a discrete glass of well-chilled fino sherry with it. My first choice would **Tesco's** £4.99 bottle of **Finest Fino**. Terrific value, great feeling to the texture of the liquid. But I have a budget to stick to and I think a certain kind of rosé is required for the lamb and so may I suggest we chill the following wine well and serve it with both courses? It is **Goats do Roam Rosé 2001** (16 points, **Oddbins**, £4.99). It is a beautifully cherry-fresh wine from the Cape and the pun, on Côtes du Rhône, is justified because the grapes in it are Rhône varieties and its producer, Charles Back of the exquisite Fairview Estate in Paarl, has 600 goats on the farm and their milk makes a large range of cheeses. Two bottles of this wine – later vintages will be every bit as tasty, I'll be bound – will cover both courses and your taste buds, handsomely. This does leave us with just tuppence to spend on the wine to go with the rhubarb. Luckily, Silvena is such a culinary genius her pud requires none. Only kidding (about her pud that is). Let me suggest, with the remarkably acidity of rhubarb, **Brown Brothers Late Harvested Orange Muscat & Flora** (16.5 points, £5.99) from Australia with its brilliant pineapple and lime fruit. It costs £5.94 at **Asda**, £5.99 at **Booths**, **Budgens**, **the Co-op**, **Majestic**, **Oddbins** and **Sainsbury's**, £6.49 at **Unwins**. For a fuller list of stockists go to the Home Page of superplonk.com and click through (or should that be lick through?).

PASTA PUTTANESCA

The name of this sauce originates from the word *'puttana'* which translated means 'whore'. It is widely believed that this dish was a favourite meal of the prostitutes in Naples, who needed something quick, hot and nourishing after their busy days of work. Whether you choose to believe that story is neither here or there, but it is certainly a curious one! What is certain though, nothing rivals a good puttanesca pasta sauce, and I hope the recipe below proves that!

200g dry pasta (penne would be good)
salt and pepper

Puttanesca sauce
20ml olive oil
4 garlic cloves, finely chopped
1 x 400g can cherry tomatoes, drained
50g pitted green olives, sliced
1 tbsp capers
1 tbsp anchovies, chopped
1/2 small red pepper, seeded and finely chopped
1/4 tsp dried chilli flakes
2 tbsp chopped oregano

For the sauce, heat the olive oil in a large pan and sweat the garlic for about 5 minutes. Add the tomatoes and cook for a further 5 minutes, then add the olives, capers, anchovies, pepper and chilli, and simmer for 15 minutes. Season to taste with salt and pepper and add the chopped oregano.

Boil the pasta in plenty of boiling salted water until al dente, then drain and mix in the puttanesca sauce. Serve at once.

COST £ 2.10

ROAST FILLET of MONKFISH
wrapped in SAGE and PARMA HAM

'Poor man's lobster', they call monkfish, and they are wrong on two counts: it doesn't taste like lobster at all, and its price now is similar to that of lobster and certainly out of reach for any 'poor man'. Today you can find monkfish anywhere, and the price is always about £12–15 a kilo. Should you order it in a restaurant then expect to pay even more, because it is a fish that, just like sea bass, has a very high price tag. It is delicious and very meaty, though, with no bones, so long as the big middle bone has been removed.

    800g monkfish tail, cut in 4 thick pieces, skin, bone and
        membrane removed
    16 large sage leaves
    4 large thin slices Parma ham
    butter
    4 tbsp dry white wine
    200g small new potatoes, scrubbed
    salt

Preheat the oven to 220°C/425°F/Gas 7.

Take each piece of monkfish and wrap around with four sage leaves, then cover and wrap in a slice of Parma ham. Secure with wooden cocktail sticks and place in a lightly buttered smallish tray with the wine.

Cook the monkfish fillets in the preheated oven for about 15 minutes until the ham is crisp and brown.

Meanwhile, cook the new potatoes in salted water for 10 minutes or more, depending on size. Drain and top with about 20g of the butter. Serve the monkfish with the buttered new potatoes.

COST £15.40

PINEAPPLE and GINGER TARTE TATIN TARTLETS with CARAMEL SAUCE

Glazed, sweet and oozing with flavour, this is a very daring alternative to the traditional apple tarte tartin. It is very important that you try and obtain the best-quality puff pastry you can, as it makes all the difference. I usually buy it from my local deli, where they make it once a week with tons of butter. When I use it in my cooking, it rises well and tastes enormously delicious.

120g puff pastry, fresh or thawed frozen
1 fresh pineapple, peeled and sliced into rings, 5mm thick
220g caster sugar
4 tbsp water
1cm piece fresh root ginger, peeled and finely grated
milk
4 tbsp crème fraîche

Preheat the oven to 220°C/425°F/Gas 7.

Roll out the puff pastry, about 1cm thick, and cut out four 6cm circles. Cover and refrigerate until ready to use.

You will only need four slices of the sliced pineapple (the rest you can keep for another use or eat fresh). Trim the four slices to the same 6cm size as the pastry circles, and cut out the hard middles.

Make the caramel sauce by cooking the sugar and water in a heavy saucepan over a medium heat for about 10–12 minutes until golden brown, taking care to not over-cook the caramel as it will burn and become very bitter.

Have four 6cm ring moulds ready and wrap them with pieces of foil to make a base. Spoon some of the caramel sauce and a pinch of the grated ginger into each, cover with a pineapple slice and top with a puff pastry circle. Repeat with all four.

Brush the pastry with some milk and bake in the preheated oven for 20–30 minutes until the pastry has risen and become golden.

To serve, remove the rings from the oven and immediately invert on to serving plates. Accompany with crème fraîche.

COST £2.20

THE WINE SELECTION

Beginning with a strumpet and ending with a tart, eh? It makes this menu seems more louche, loose, than in fact it is. Pasta 'puttanesca' ('whore-like' in Italian) is more accurately etymologised by Silvena than even that authoritative word scientist John Ayto in his splendid *A Gourmet's Guide – Food and Drink from A to Z* (OUP, £6.99). John reckons pasta puttanesca owes its name to the 'pungency' of its sauce but he is wrong. It owes its name more or less as my companion-chef describes, except that it was Roman whores greater gourmettes by far than their fellow-slatterns in Naples – who inspired the dish because they required something to keep their strength up and also to perfume their breath so they could instantly repel clients to whose fancy they did not take. Undoubtedly, the girls drank Frascati with their pasta, as it is refreshing and cheap and the house white of Rome. Frascati is the principal white wine of the Latium region (in which Rome sits) and its production, in the Alban Hills, though widespread, does include some notable specimens. There is one such in Radcliffe's Regional Classics – the new **Thresher** range of wines. **Radcliffe's Frascati 2002 (16 points, £4.99)** is clean and crisp with fine touches of citrus to very dry, subtle peach and pineapple. **Tesco's** brand, the so-called **Finest Frascati Classico Superiore 2002 (15.5 points, £4.99)** is also good, showing class, weight and wit.

Now either of these wines would certainly see you through the next course, that splendid monkfish wrapped in sage and Parma ham. 'Poor man's lobster', they used to call monkfish, says Silvena, and the reason is that before Silvena was born the fish was considered so ugly it was never put on retail sale but sold to restaurants and fish bars, so it was always cheap, and it was chopped up and each morsel passed off as a scampi tail (fried). Once the superior qualities of this marvellous fish were more widely (and less fraudulently) recognised, beginning in the late sixties, it become almost a delicacy – though it is still as ugly to look at as ever (having an alien appearance, with its huge mouth and bulbous eyes, of something from a *Men in Black*

movie). This particular recipe suggests an Italian wine and though a Frascati is not inappropriate I can suggest other, and more richly endowed candidates, such as **Boekenhoutskloof Sémillon 2002**, on sale at **Oddbins Fine Wine** branches around £14 (rating **16.5 points** decanted 7–8 hours before drinking), Sémillons from Australia, white Graves from Bordeaux, Chardonnay from Apulia or Sicily (Trulli and Planeta are the names to look for), and also Chilean Sauvignon Blanc. Specifically, in the last instance, **Santa Rita Reserva Casablanca Valley Sauvignon Blanc 2003** (**16 points**, **£6.99**, **Majestic**) which flaunts beautifully crisp, fresh, under-ripe gooseberry with citrus and a faraway hint of spicy pineapple. On the other hand, consider chilling a lighter style of red. Dare I suggest a Beaujolais? I have vilified this mostly wretched wine for some decades now but occasionally a decent specimen surfaces and again Thresher has one such. **Radcliffe's Beaujolais 2001** (**16 points**, **£4.99**) is brilliantly screwcapped – which all Beaujolais ought to be – and what a difference it makes to the wine. All the tannins are retained and the plummy fruit is harvest fresh and tangy with a hint of wild raspberry. It is the most concentrated Beaujolais I've tasted from producer Georges Duboeuf since he treated me to an old Morgon a decade ago which tasted like a first-rate Chambolle-Musigny.

The pud presents another problem – the caramel sauce with the ginger. The sweet wine to go with these ingredients needs good acidity to cope here, mere sweetness is insufficient, and so **Brown Brothers Late Harvested Orange Muscat & Flora 2002** (**16.5 points**) from Australia is my first choice for it is intensely honied with pineapple and lime acids. It costs £5.94 at **Asda**, £5.99 at **Booths, Budgens, the Co-op, Majestic, Oddbins** and **Sainsbury**, £6.49 at **Unwins**. It is also available at **Adnams, Rodney Densem, Charles Hennings, www.everywine.co.uk, SH Jones, Noble Rot of Bromsgrove, Peckham & Rye, Penistone Court of Barnsley**, and **Chris Piper**.

SEARED SARDINES with TOMATO and AVOCADO SALSA

Sardines are wonderful small fish with a strong flavour, the ultimate old-fashioned feast. Sardines are something we absolutely adore to have when on holiday in France or Spain, yet we seem to be reluctant to cook them at home, despite being excellent value and delicious in taste. When buying sardines, look for a skin that is fresh, shiny and silver-blue, that is firm to the touch, and the eye must look bright.

8 sardines
1 tbsp plain flour
5 tbsp olive oil

Salsa
3 large tomatoes, skinned and seeded
1 large avocado, stoned and peeled
1 red onion, finely chopped
1 garlic clove, minced
1 small red chilli, seeded and chopped
5 tbsp chopped coriander
4 tbsp green olives, pitted and chopped
juice of 1 lime
salt and pepper

Make the salsa first. Dice the flesh of the tomatoes and avocado into small squares. Place in a bowl and add the onion, garlic, chilli, coriander, olives and lime juice. Season and add more lime juice if required. Mix well and keep aside.

To prepare the fish, you can have a go at filleting them yourself. Here is how. Remove the heads from the sardines. Remove the backbone from each fish by making cuts along both sides of the backbone, all along its length. Carefully take out the bone and as many of the fine bones as you can as well.

Dust each sardine fillet with flour and pan-fry in very hot oil, for no longer than 30 seconds each side. Drain well.

Divide the tomato and avocado salsa between four plates and top with four sardine fillets.

COST £ 4.80

BASIL RISOTTO with YELLOW PEPPER SAUCE

A delicious risotto to remind us of what flavours are to come with spring and summer! Try to find the best-quality basil; preferably visit a farmers' market, where it will be on sale, just freshly picked.

30g butter
1 onion, finely chopped
2 garlic cloves, minced
180g arborio rice
1 litre chicken stock (see page 197), simmering
2 tbsp freshly grated Parmesan
2 large bunches basil, leaves only
salt and pepper

Yellow pepper sauce
2 large yellow peppers
2 tbsp olive oil

Preheat the oven to 200°C/400°F/Gas 6.

To prepare the yellow pepper sauce, roast the peppers in the preheated oven until their skins have browned and are coming off, about 25 minutes. Peel them completely, seed and core them, and place the flesh in a food processor, along with the olive oil. Blend to a purée, and keep warm until ready to use.

Melt the butter in a heavy-based saucepan, and cook the onion and garlic until soft but not brown. Add the rice and stir to coat with the butter. Start adding ladlefuls of hot chicken stock to the rice and keep doing so until all is absorbed and until all the stock has been used. The rice should be cooked but still have a bit of bite to it, al dente.

Add the Parmesan and gently mix in the basil leaves, without bruising them. Season to taste. Serve the risotto with some yellow pepper sauce around it.

COST £6.70

LAVENDER and ALMOND PANNACOTTA, with BERRY SAUCE

If you have made the previous Party Paupers pannacotta recipes, you will know by now that this is easy but at the same time a very impressive dessert. The lavender, with its regal flavour, beautifully complements the creamy and velvety textured pannacotta.

2 gelatine leaves
300ml double cream
100g shelled whole almonds, toasted
50g caster sugar
2 tbsp fresh lavender leaves and flowers

Berry sauce
100g berries (frozen are fine)
2 tbsp caster sugar

Soak the gelatine in some cold water to soften.

Place the cream, almonds and sugar in a medium saucepan, and simmer for 2 minutes. Remove from the heat, add the lavender, and leave to infuse for an hour.

Reheat the cream gently. Add the softened and drained gelatine to the cream, and stir in well until dissolved. Pass through a fine sieve, discarding the almonds and lavender, and pour into four pannacotta moulds. Place in the refrigerator to set for at least 5 hours or preferably overnight.

To make the berry sauce, use any berries you can get such as raspberries. Fresh would be too expensive, so go for frozen, which will do just fine. Place the berries in a small saucepan and add 2 tbsp water. Simmer for 5–7 minutes, then add the sugar and leave to cool. When ready to use, pass the sauce through a fine sieve.

Unmould each pannacotta into the middle of a serving plate, as described on page 38, and drizzle around the berry sauce.

COST £4.80

THE WINE SELECTION

I know the perfect wine to go with those sardines. Now I know you will
retort 'So you bloomin' well should since it's your job to be privy to such
things', but rarely does a wine sing out so loudly and resolutely to be the
prime candidate to accompany those fish as **Villa Maria Private Bin
Riesling 2002.** This New Zealand wine, rating **16 points** and costing
around £6.50 at **Waitrose**, has delightful thick melon fruit with lively
lemon (with a touch of gooseberry about it). It is still perky, still babyish.
It is a screwcapped wine, so it can confidently be stored in a cool dark
spot for up to ten years further (at which time 18.5 points should be
attained). A basil risotto with yellow pepper sauce, especially since
Parmesan cheese is around, requires a red wine. And once again I feel
my hand unerringly alighting on a contender clamouring to be
considered above all others. It is **Torres Manso de Velasco 2000, (18.5
points, £16.50** approx.) at **Ipswich Wines and Beers**, **Thomas Peatling**,
Harrods, **Portland Wine Company**, **Roberts and Speight**, **Sandhams
Wine Merchants**, **Soho Wine Supply**, and **J. Wadsworth**. For fuller
contact details of Manso de Velasco see the Home Page of
superplonk.com). This Chilean Cabernet Sauvignon blows my budget
sky-high but it is one of those masterpieces every bit as satisfying as a
Mozart piano sonata. As a liquid it surely seems to be composed of
something other than mere grapes. Something so svelte has come from
pressed berries? What comes to mind is *Henry IV*'s 'smooth as oil, soft
as young down'. Overall, leaving aside the little avenues of exploration
afforded by its subtle complexities, the wine offers suggestions of creamy
coffee with tannins like taffeta. Risotto appreciates softness in its wine.

As for that lavender and almond pannacotta, something altogether
sweeter is required, of course, and I have no hesitation in demanding of
my butler that he bring up from the cellar (or he gets on his bike and
visits one of the 60 branches of **Sainsbury's** which stocks it) **Torres
Muscatel Oro** from Spain in the 50cl bottle. Rating **16 points** and costing
£6.99, this unctuously honied wine has stunning custardy fruit with a
hint of toasty raspberry. It is sheer luxury and brings to mind words like
satin-sheeted, plumply rich, paradisiacally perfumed, sybaritically
sensational.

Menu 6   WARM KING PRAWN and ENDIVE SALAD
FRICASSEE of CHICKEN and GREEN OLIVES
PEACHES in FILO PASTRY with MASCARPONE SAUCE

WARM KING PRAWN and ENDIVE SALAD
with BLOOD ORANGES, PECANS and POMEGRANATE

A luxurious, crisp and very citrussy salad with which to celebrate early spring! The lively colours and innovative combination of flavours are a reminder of what is to come in spring. Pomegranates are still around, although not local of course. Dried fruits, such as cherries, are a good substitute.

2 large blood oranges, peeled and segmented
200g green curly endive leaves, washed
1 red onion, sliced
2 tbsp olive oil
12 king prawns, peeled, tail left intact
salt and pepper
40g shelled pecans, coarsely chopped
1 pomegranate, seeded

Orange vinaigrette
2 tbsp olive oil
2 tbsp orange juice
2 tbsp red wine vinegar
1 tsp finely chopped coriander

Combine the oranges, endive leaves and red onion in a salad bowl.

Heat the olive oil in a heavy-based pan, and when very hot cook the king prawns, for about 2 minutes on each side, until brown. Season with salt and pepper and keep warm.

To make the vinaigrette, combine all the ingredients, season with salt and pepper, and mix well.

Serve the salad on to four plates, adding the pecans. Top each portion with three king prawns. Drizzle with the dressing and sprinkle with the pomegranate seeds.

COST £8.30

FRICASSEE of CHICKEN and GREEN OLIVES

Fricassee is one of my favourite dishes, rather comforting and satisfying at the same time. It is a very East European dish, and I was brought up on it. It can be vegetarian as well, if you use vegetables only. The secret of a light and creamy fricassee is the sauce.

1 chicken, about 1kg in weight
1 onion, chopped
2 tbsp olive oil
3 leeks, white part only, sliced
2 carrots, sliced
2 celery stalks, sliced
100ml dry white wine
300ml chicken stock (see page 197)
10 cloves
2 sprigs parsley
5 fresh bay leaves
salt and pepper
45g butter
2 tbsp plain flour
3 egg yolks
150ml single cream
2 tbsp chopped thyme leaves
100g green olives, pitted and sliced

Preheat the oven to 160°C/325°F/Gas 3. Cut the chicken into quarters.

In a heavy casserole, brown the onion in the olive oil, then add the leek, carrot and celery, and sauté for 5 minutes. Arrange the chicken pieces over the vegetables, then pour in the wine and chicken stock. Add the cloves, parsley and bay leaves, and season.

Place the casserole in the preheated oven and cook for about 1¹/₂ hours. When ready, take out of the oven and keep warm. Pour out the cooking liquid, strain, and keep aside.

In a shallow pan, melt the butter, add the flour and cook until light brown. Gradually add most of the cooking liquid, stirring until the sauce is thick and smooth. Mix the egg yolks and cream and add to the fricassee sauce. Do not let this boil, just simmer gently.

Add the thyme and green olives to the sauce, and pour into the casserole with the chicken. Simmer for just 2–3 minutes, then serve with plain boiled white rice.

COST £8.40

PEACHES in FILO PASTRY with PECANS, MASCARPONE and MAPLE SYRUP SAUCE

Peaches are available imported, and in combination with mascarpone and maple syrup, make a robust and unusual dessert. When using filo pastry keep all the filo sheets under a damp cloth as they dry out very quickly. Filo is sold in most supermarkets fresh or frozen. It is a pastry that is very easy to use.

   6 large sheets filo pastry
   2 tbsp melted butter
   4 tbsp caster sugar
   60g shelled pecans, toasted and finely chopped
   1 large peach, skinned, pitted and quartered
   4 tbsp mascarpone cheese
   4 tbsp maple syrup
   2 tbsp golden icing sugar

Preheat the oven to 180°C/350°F/Gas 4.

Lay out one sheet of filo pastry and brush well with the melted butter, then sprinkle with sugar and nuts. Repeat this with the rest of the filo sheets on top of the first layer. Cut the stack of filo, lengthwise, into four equal strips.

Place a piece of peach, 1 tbsp mascarpone and 1 tbsp maple syrup on each of the strips. Roll up roly-poly style and place on a baking sheet.

Bake in the preheated oven for 15 minutes until golden brown. Serve dusted with some golden icing sugar.

COST £3.20

THE WINE SELECTION

So many traps here to snare the unwary wine-matcher! That blood orange juice, those pomegranate seeds, that red wine vinegar – and that's just the first hurdle for starters. Even the endive here adds its own peculiar piquancy. My instinct is to demand a fino or manzanilla sherry be brought. Both, it can be argued, are the same thing but the difference is that the first does come from Jerez – the corruption into English of which gives us the word 'sherry' – whilst the second is also a fino but it is different, sassier, because it is made only in the neighbouring town of Sanlucar de Barrameda and acquires something of the neighbourhood's chutzpah (Jerez being somewhat sedate). It is less brusque than fino and in the town the locals drink it with grilled prawns and the local hams and, each in its own way, these make splendid marriages. It is, then, manzanilla which I recommend with the first course and specifically **Tesco's** so-called **Finest Manzanilla Extra Dry** (**16.5 points**, £4.99) which I enjoyed a lot of whilst reading J. L. Carr's magnificent novel *A Day in Summer* (a novel like John Cowper Powys or D. H. Lawrence rewritten by Barbara Pym and so what we get is a comic masterpiece overflowing with rural indignities and black-comedic insights into the English condition). This wine is one of the most individual and delicious manzanillas I've tasted. The aroma is of black olive. The fruit in the mouth recalls almond with some kind of far-distant hint of fruit (damson perhaps, though this is far too sweet a metaphor), and the texture has a chalky chewiness of extraordinary subtlety yet affirmativeness. It will be superb with Silvena's prawns which in their own way have a sort of Andalusian touch (the blood orange juice for a start). Sherry like this acquires its unique style because it attracts a strange yeast called 'flor' which infiltrates the wine some months after fermentation (and after fortification to 15% alcohol, for manzanilla is a fortified wine). It settles on the surface of the wine in its big barrels (which maintain a gap, unlike normal table wine barrels which are bunged tight, to encourage the growth which

demands air to flourish) like a faux butter spread. It looks most
unappetising (and indeed is so to taste). Now I appreciate splashing out
nigh on a fiver for the first course is half my budget gone but I suggest
you only serve four small glasses of the wine and so in fact we've only
spend a quarter of my budget (and you get to keep the half left over for
another day, as the wine will keep for a couple of weeks in the fridge).
The second course, that fricassee of chicken with green olives, is also a
touch tricky because of the last-named ingredient. True, the beautiful
smoothness, couthness, of the creamy sauce mollifies the effects of the
olive but we must tread carefully here. A dilemma presents itself and
each drinker must solve it in his and her own way: do we serve white
wine or red or, indeed, rosé? You have, I suspect, already guessed the
direction this is leading and it is indeed to a pink wine. I have in
mind Chilean or Hungarian or Italian Cabernet Sauvignon rosé which
has more aroma, weight, and richness than most other rosés. **Inycon
Cabernet Sauvignon Rosé 2002 (15.5 points, £4.99** at **Sainsbury's)** from
Sicily fits the bill perfectly, being a deliciously dry cherry/plum rosé of
elegance and purpose. Over the budget? Yep. But we can, as an
alternative, stay within it if we chill, judiciously, a couple of bottles of
Asda's South African Pinotage 2002 (16 points, £3.22). This has
succulence yet style, offering rubbery plums, pert blackberries, a hint of
prune and lashings of tannin. A touch exotic, very warm yet not soppy,
this wine will handle that chicken and those olives with classy aplomb.
This leaves nothing for the pudding wine. Oh to hell with budgets!
How can we economise when we have those peaches on our plates? It
is a sumptuous dessert and it deserves a sumptuous wine and since we
have been shopping in **Tesco** we may as well tarry there. And again we
have a choice (of half bottles): the own-label **Finest Botrytis Sémillon
2000 (16 points, £4.99)** from Australia is superbly ripe yet gorgeously
acidic, whilst **Muscat de Beaumes de Venise (16 points, £4.49)** shows
ripe pineapple, honey and a touch of toffee apple.

ASPARAGUS with BALSAMIC BUTTER and PECORINO

Without a doubt, asparagus is the most delectable of spring vegetables, and this is the perfect spring dish: crisp asparagus served with lashings of melted balsamic butter and shavings of pecorino cheese. It is rustic, simple and easy to prepare, and it has surprising flavour. Asparagus should not be over-cooked. If you want, you can substitute the pecorino cheese with Parmesan.

2 bunches medium-thick asparagus stalks
salt and pepper
80g butter
4 tbsp balsamic vinegar
50g Pecorino cheese shavings

Break the tough ends off the asparagus and discard. Trim the asparagus, using a vegetable peeler. Lightly blanch the asparagus in some boiling salted water, no longer than 5 minutes. Drain and keep aside on a warm place.

Melt the butter over a low heat in a large frying pan and add the balsamic vinegar. Toss the asparagus in the butter and balsamic mixture and cook for just 2 more minutes. Season to taste.

Serve immediately, while hot, topped generously with the pecorino shavings.

Cost £5.85

'NAKED' RAVIOLI with GORGONZOLA

The ravioli are literally naked – free form, and not wrapped in pasta – and they are very easy to prepare. Once you have mastered these ravioli you will never look back. They could be prepared earlier and stored in the fridge until ready to use. This dish is very much about spring with its strong seasonal flavours. I like to use the sweeter Gorgonzola, known as 'dolce'. If you can only find the very strong-flavoured Gorgonzola, then use mascarpone cheese instead.

> 200g fresh spinach, washed and cleaned
> 200g fresh Swiss chard, washed and cleaned
> salt and pepper
> 150g ricotta cheese
> 150g Gorgonzola dolce cheese
> 3 egg yolks
> 150g Parmesan, freshly grated
> 1/2 nutmeg, freshly grated
> 100g plain flour
> 200g butter
> 20 sage leaves, finely chopped

Place the spinach and chard in a large saucepan of water and bring to the boil. Add some salt and cook for 10 minutes. Drain, squeeze dry, and chop finely on a chopping board.

Place the chopped greens in a large bowl, with the ricotta, Gorgonzola, egg yolks, two-thirds of the Parmesan, and season with nutmeg and salt and pepper to taste. Mix very well, using a wooden spoon.

To cook the ravioli, bring a large saucepan of water to the boil. Spread the flour on a board. Take a heaped tablespoon of the cheese mixture and roll it into a small ball. Flour the ball evenly and repeat the same with the rest of the mixture. Drop the balls, five or six at a time only, into the boiling water and let them cook for 30 seconds when they will rise to the top. Remove using a slotted spoon.

Melt the butter gently over a low heat and then coat the drained ravioli. Serve immediately, adding the rest of the Parmesan and the sage leaves.

COST £8.80

GENNARO'S CHOCOLATE and RED WINE CAKE

This recipe, I have to admit, is not mine. It is taken from *Passione* by Gennaro Contaldo, truly an exciting discovery. Chocolate and red wine, the perfect partnership. Best served with some thick cream.

    200g butter, softened, plus extra for greasing
    250g caster sugar
    4 eggs, beaten
    25g cocoa powder
    250g plain flour
    1 tsp baking powder
    100ml red wine
    1/2 tsp vanilla extract
    150g plain chocolate drops

Preheat the oven to 180°C/350°F/Gas 4 and lightly grease a loose-bottomed 20cm cake tin.

Cream the butter and sugar together until light and fluffy. Gradually beat in the eggs. Then sift in the cocoa powder, flour and baking powder. Mix in the red wine and vanilla, and then fold in the chocolate drops.

Pour the mixture into the prepared cake tin and bake for about 1 hour, until a skewer inserted in the centre comes out clean. Remove from the oven and allow to cool in the tin before turning out.

COST £4.40

THE WINE SELECTION

The way it works with my culinary seductress, that co-author of mine, is that we don't, as some might think, spend all our time hob-nobbing. Oh no. She has her state-of-the-art kitchen in South London and I have my wine cupboard in North London, and now and then we meet in the middle. We correspond by e-mail most of the time and for this menu, before she sent it to me, Silvena telephoned and told me she was going easy on me and planning an Italian vegetarian spread. I was delighted. Especially when the dear sweet thing added that even the pudding was going to be a cakewalk for me. 'It is, my dear,' she said brazenly, 'going to be made with 100 millilitres of red wine.' And then the details of the dishes arrived and I'm tearing out my hair (note the use of the singular here). My first-choice wine to go with asparagus with balsamic butter is a single-estate German Riesling Spätlese or one of the 2001, 2002 or 2003 vintage own-label **Alsace Gewürztraminers** at **Tesco**, **Sainsbury's** and **Safeway** (all **16 points** plus and around **six quid**). However, I have another idea. It is **Tesco's** impressive wine box, **Argentinian White**, which is 3 litres of non-vintage, **16-point** wine. It has a delightful grapefruit and honey edge, which should work with the asparagus. At £11.49 the box, this wine really is a steal. It works out at 47p a glass, or the equivalent of £2.87 a bottle. This leaves me sufficient funds, if you drink a bottle's worth of the box, to find two bottles of red for the ravioli and the wine has to be **Asda's** own-label non-vintage **Claret** (**16 points**, £2.58) with its savourily classy berries and accompanying tannins. Two bottles should do you nicely with perhaps a glass left over for Gennaro's chocolate cake. You could even splash out on a third bottle and use some of it in the recipe. Of course that claret won't go with the chocolate cake but a budget is a budget, n'est-ce pas ? However, in a spirit of goodwill let me offer a wine which will go with it: **Somerfield's** sweetly striking Aussie **Campbells Rutherglen Muscat** (**16.5 points**, £7.49 the half bottle). It is as thick as axle grease but a million times more sweetly lubricational (with its sweet peach fruit) and more than fair dinkum, whatever that means, with that chocolate cake.

BULGARIAN NETTLE 'KASHA' with POACHED EGG

Time to venture into the countryside for some 'free' food. Nettles, just out, grow almost everywhere, have therapeutic qualities and represent great food value. Pick the very top, young leaves, which can also be used in salads. Handling nettles is supposed to be good for rheumatism and I, for one, pick nettles without using gloves. Nettles can be cooked like spinach, but are best eaten in the beginning of the season, while they are tender. The eating of kasha goes back many centuries. In this recipe, the Slavic term 'kasha' refers to a texture rather than a particular ingredient, but most often kasha is a dish prepared using buckwheat groats.

> 1 carrier-bagful of nettles
> 50g butter
> 1 onion, finely chopped
> 2 large garlic cloves, finely chopped
> salt and pepper
> pinch of cayenne pepper
> 1 litre hot vegetable stock (see page 197)
> 5 tbsp cooked pudding rice
> 4 eggs

Wash the nettles and discard the tough bits.

Melt the butter in a large saucepan and sweat the onion and garlic without colouring. Season with salt, black pepper and cayenne pepper. Add the nettles and sauté briefly. Now add the stock and cooked rice, and simmer for about 10 minutes.

Liquidise the soup, return at once to the pan and bring to the boil, stirring continuously. Almost immediately crack open the eggs one by one and drop into the hot soup, stirring very gently. The eggs will poach themselves in the hot liquid. Serve at once while hot with an egg in each portion.

Free, or the cost of 4 eggs!

PEARL BARLEY 'RISOTTO' with LOBSTER and CHILLI

There is only one way to eat lobster and that's cooking it from raw! Taste and quality suffer a great deal if you buy one that is frozen or ready cooked. You can order from your local fishmonger or visit your local fish market as I did, though I am lucky, as mine is Billingsgate. Expect to pay around £13.50 to £17.00 per kilo.

1 x 800g raw lobster
salt and pepper
200g pearl barley
2 shallots, finely chopped
1 garlic clove, finely chopped
4 tbsp olive oil
½ tsp chilli flakes
1 litre hot chicken stock (see page 197)

To cook the lobster from live, put in the freezer 2 hours before cooking, which will kill it painlessly. Have a large pan with boiling salted water ready and add the lobster. Bring it to the boil again and let it simmer for about 7 minutes. This way the lobster will still be partly raw and will enable you, when the lobster is cool, to get the meat out of the shell. The meat is in the tail and the claws, discard the rest. Cut the meat into small chunks.

To cook the barley, sauté the shallots and garlic in the olive oil, add the chilli flakes, and cook until all is translucent and fragrant. Add the barley and stir until well coated with oil. Increase the heat and start adding small ladlefuls of hot stock, bringing it all to the boil. Reduce the heat to very low and simmer, stirring constantly, adding more stock as the previous addition is absorbed (just like a risotto). Cook until the barley is soft, about 10–12 minutes. Add the lobster meat and simmer for a further 2–3 minutes. Season to taste, and serve hot.

COST £14.80

PAVLOVA with VANILLA-GLAZED RHUBARB

The good weather has arrived, and here is a foretaste of the summer. Rhubarb is the only home-grown fruit we have at this time of the year. I love using it in savoury dishes as well as in puddings.

6 egg whites
pinch of salt
360g caster sugar
2 tsp cornflour
1 tsp white wine vinegar

Rhubarb
200g rhubarb, washed, trimmed and cut into 4cm pieces
50g caster sugar
juice of 1 lemon
1 vanilla pod, split lengthways

Preheat the oven to 180°C/350°F/Gas 4, and line a tray with baking paper.

Put the egg whites in a large bowl with the pinch of salt and start whisking in the sugar, 1 tbsp at a time. Keep whisking the whites until glossy and stiff. Lastly whisk in the cornflour and vinegar.

Mould the meringue on to the paper-lined tray in the shape of a large circle, smoothing the top and sides. Bake the meringue for 5 minutes then turn down the oven to 120°C/250°F/Gas 1/2 and cook for about 1 1/2 hours. The finished meringue should be crunchy-crusted and marshmallow-centred.

For the glazed rhubarb, combine the rhubarb, sugar, lemon juice, vanilla seeds and pod with 200ml water in a saucepan. Simmer until the sugar dissolves, and cook until the rhubarb is tender, about 5 minutes. Remove the fruit from the juices with a slotted spoon and cool. Keep the juices aside, and remove the vanilla pod.

To assemble, place the fruit in the middle of the pavlova and serve immediately. Pour some juice round it.

COST £3.40

THE WINE SELECTION

When I was a child the lady who lived next door always picked the nettles growing in our garden with my mother's blessing though, naturally, I assumed the neighbour was a witch with a secret recipe which also involved bats' eyes and frogs' tongues. Silvena's nettle soup, I note, lacks these ingredients and thus I am able, far more readily, to think of what kind of wine might be appropriate for it. My suggestion is, then, that when the other couple arrive you open a bottle of **Araldica Moscato Spumante (Sainsbury's, 16 points, £2.99)** to whet the whistle. This delightful light bubbly from Italy has joyous sweet melon fruit with a hint of custard but a glass or two of this is a perfect aperitif and it will set up the soup perfectly. With this you open one bottle (you need to buy two) of **Sainsbury's** non-vintage **Romanian Pinot Noir (£2.99, 15.5 points)** with its lingering chewiness of plum and cherry and light tannins. The soup and wine will make beautiful love together (old Bulgarian saying). The second bottle of Rumanian Pinot – I'm sorry, Silvena, but I couldn't find a Bulgarian wine for your feast but surely this is the next best thing, indeed it is much the best thing of all – you thoroughly chill and serve with the lobster thingy. No white wine within my budget will work with such a luxurious dish but this Pinot is perfect – for it is a most accommodating wine.

As for the pavlova with poached rhubarb, well...having spent £8.97 already you have only £1.03 left for a pud wine. But then if you have been following this book's suggestions you already have half a bottle of **Moscatel de Valencia** left over from a previous dinner-party menu and so you use that and put £1.03 in the kitty for your next culinary bash (don't worry, I won't let you forget). Of course, with money no object then I suggest, with the lobster, **Volnay 1er Cru Les Fermiets Domaine Annick Parent 2000 (16 points, £22.45, Haynes, Hanson & Clark)**. Yes, it's a red wine but nicely gamey and nicely chilled it will do...well...very nicely. And for the pud? **Oddbins** has **D'Arenberg Noble Riesling McLaren Vale 1999 (17 points, £10.99** the half bottle) from Australia. It is strikingly original, like vinified tarte tatin and will do that pavlova proud.

PIEROGI FILLED with CREAM CHEESE, POTATO and CHIVES   *Menu 9*
UZBEK LAMB with CUMIN, CORIANDER and WATERCRESS
BANANA BAILEY'S CUSTARD

PIEROGI FILLED with CREAM CHEESE, POTATO and CHIVES

Small parcels of dough stuffed with various fillings are a component of almost every cuisine of the globe: think of the Chinese dim sum, the Japanese gyoza, or Indian samosas. 'Pierogi' – also known as 'piroshki' – are ravioli-like filled pastries and are typical of Eastern European cuisine. They are perfect for a snack, canapé or hot entrée.

300g plain flour
2 eggs
salt and pepper
80g butter
4 tsp soured cream

Filling
2 large potatoes, boiled, skinned and mashed
200g cream cheese
bunch each of spring onions and chives, finely chopped

In a food processor mix the flour, eggs, a pinch of salt and 4–5 tbsp water to get a smooth dough. Work the dough on a board until you are happy with it: it should be smooth and elastic. Divide in two parts and roll each piece into a thin sheet on a floured board. Use a pasta machine (if you have one), to achieve a ravioli-like thickness.

To make the filling, mix everything together and season well.

Arrange a spoonful of the filling along one edge of a piece of dough, 3cm from the edge. Fold over and cut into a semi-circle using a pastry cutter or glass. Press the edges of the dough together. Repeat with the rest until all the ingredients are used up.

To cook, boil a large pan of water, and cook the pierogi as you would noodles, covered, so that they will steam. When the pierogi rise to the top, they are done. You can serve now simply with melted butter on top, which is the traditional way and they are absolutely delicious. But I like to do something different. Sauté the pierogi in the butter until lightly browned, then serve immediately with soured cream.

COST £3.65

UZBEK LAMB with CUMIN, CORIANDER and WATERCRESS

This is very much a one-pot meal, prepared with the freshest seasonal ingredients. Use spring lamb, which is in season, and crunchy, peppery watercress. The lamb is simmered with spring vegetables and beautifully spiced with the traditional Uzbek seasoning – a combination of 'zira' or cumin seeds, cayenne and crushed coriander.

4 tbsp vegetable oil
800g neck of lamb, cut into small cubes
1 large onion, finely chopped
200g baby carrots, trimmed and washed
1 large red pepper, seeded and cut into strips
1 tsp cumin seeds, lightly toasted
1 tsp coriander seeds, crushed
6 whole black peppercorns
1/2 tsp sweet Hungarian paprika
1/2 tsp cayenne pepper
300ml lamb stock (see page 199)
100g new season baby potatoes, washed
5 garlic cloves, minced
salt and pepper
large bunch of watercress, washed and trimmed

Heat the oil in a large heavy saucepan, then add the meat, onion, carrots and pepper strips, and sauté until golden brown. Stir in the spices and most of the stock. Cover and simmer gently for about an hour.

Now add the potatoes, garlic and the rest of the stock to just about cover the potatoes, and cook for another 20 minutes. Season to taste, then stir in the watercress and turn off the heat. Serve almost immediately, accompanied by pitta bread.

COST £13.80

BANANA BAILEY'S CUSTARD

Light and very delicious! Use whatever alcohol you have in your cupboard – maybe rum or sherry – but Bailey's makes this pudding very sexy! You can also prepare this dessert in small individual glasses.

    500ml milk
    2 eggs, separated
    60g caster sugar
    1¹/₂ tbsp powdered gelatine
    4 soft bananas, peeled and mashed
    5 tbsp Bailey's Irish Cream
    80g shelled pistachio nuts, chopped

Bring the milk gently to the boil in a saucepan over a medium heat. At the same time, whisk the egg yolks and sugar together in a bowl until pale and creamy. As soon as the milk has boiled, pour it slowly over the egg yolk mixture and blend well. Put the bowl over a pan of hot water and stir until the custard thickens and coats the back of a spoon.

Meanwhile soak the gelatine in 4 tbsp cold water, drain and add it to the hot custard. Stir in the mashed bananas and the Bailey's. Add more Bailey's if a stronger taste is desired, I always do....Leave to cool for about 15 minutes.

Whip the egg whites until stiff. Fold them gently into the cooled custard. Pour the mixture into a medium glass container (or individual glasses) and leave to set.

Sprinkle with pistachio nuts just before serving.

COST £ 2.20

THE WINE SELECTION

What an extraordinarily cosmopolitan menu this is, and the touch of
Bailey's liquor in the pud even smuggles in a wittily Irish twist.
What, to start with, can I find to sympathetically lubricate the
passage of pierogi (filled with cream cheese, potato and chives) down
the throat? I incline to a white wine from Hungary called **Margaret
Island White Country Wine 2001 (Sainsbury's, 14 points, £2.99)**,
which is fresh and crisp to finish but in-between gives the drinker's
palate a fair old wallop of exotic-edged fruitiness. This is essential to
combat what is a fairly rich dish. A bottle will do the four of you
nicely.

To follow, with the Uzbek lamb with cumin, coriander and
watercress, we need to be wary. Coriander and cumin are Middle
Eastern flavourings, and they confer a lovely gaminess to the stew, a
genuine hint of the casbah, I would say, and we need two bottles of
**Cuvée Chasseur, Vin de Pays de l'Hérault 2002 (Waitrose, 16 points,
£2.99)**. This is a gorgeously adventurous blend of 55% Grenache,
25% Carignan and 20% Merlot, and is made by a large, but
extremely forward-looking, wine co-op between Carcassonne and
Béziers in the Midi. Frankly, I regard it as one of the UK's most
absurdly under-priced red wines. It is classy, dry and very well
balanced and excellent from nose to throat.

What have we spent thus far? I make it £8.97 and with our £1.03
change we cannot, I am afraid, advance the cause of that banana
Bailey's custard dessert. If you have, however, been trying out other
menus before this one, you will have stashed away **Safeway's,
Tesco's, Sainsbury's** or **Asda's Moscatel de Valencia (£3.99** or less) in
the fridge with half of its contents still to be poured. A small glass
with the custard will round off the meal nicely – and your waistline.

SORREL OMELETTE

Now that you have mastered the art of picking and cooking nettles (see page 132), here is another wild edible leaf to go roaming about in the countryside for – sorrel. This is a perennial herb, almost as common as nettles, and similar in appearance to spinach, only its leaves are larger. Its taste is slightly lemony and it can be used raw in salads or cooked in soups and sauces. When picking, look for shiny and firm leaves. The best time to pick is in late spring, as later on in summer sorrel flowers and leaves become tougher.

> ½ carrier-bagful of sorrel leaves
> 50g butter
> 8 eggs
> salt and pepper
> 2 tbsp milk or single cream (optional)

Discard the sorrel stalks and wash the leaves thoroughly. Chop the leaves roughly and sauté in about 15g of the butter for a few minutes until soft. The sorrel becomes very dark green when cooked. Set aside and keep warm.

Now to make the omelettes, beat the eggs, then season well and add the milk or cream if using. Heat a quarter of the remaining butter in a scrupulously clean non-stick pan. Pour in a quarter of the egg mixture and, using a fork, draw the edges to the centre as soon as they begin to set. When the omelette is cooked, place some sorrel in the middle and fold it in three. Repeat the same with the remaining ingredients until you have four omelettes.

The cost of 8 eggs

CUMIN and CARDAMOM SCENTED SPRING LAMB FILLET with ENGLISH PEAS

Try and get the best and most succulent spring lamb for this recipe. You can find it at farmers' markets or order from your local butcher. The spices added to it are very delicate, adding an exotic perfume. The flavours are reminiscent of the Mediterranean. English peas are just beginning to appear.

1 x 400g lamb tenderloin
¼ tsp ground cinnamon
¼ tsp crushed black pepper
½ tsp ground cumin
½ tsp ground cardamom
¼ tsp ground coriander
¼ tsp salt
5 tbsp olive oil
200g podded English peas
15g butter
handful of mint leaves

To prepare the lamb, combine the cinnamon, pepper, cumin, cardamom, coriander and salt in a bowl. Season the lamb loin with the spice rub and place in the fridge for about 4 hours.

To cook the lamb, sauté it in the olive oil over a medium heat for about 8 minutes each side, or longer if you like it well done. Reserve any cooking juices. Keep the lamb in a warm place, until ready to serve.

Bring a small saucepan of water to the boil, and cook the podded peas for just 3–4 minutes. Drain and keep warm.

In another small pan melt the butter and sauté most of the mint leaves until just wilted, then add the drained peas. Sauté for a further 3 minutes and add the meat juices.

To serve, place some peas and cooking juice in the centre of each plate. Cut the loin into 16 slices, season to taste and arrange on top of the peas. Decorate with mint leaves.

COST £15.80

ORANGE ISRAELI COUSCOUS PUDDING

Israeli couscous is available in delicatessens and better supermarkets. It is a pearl-like grain, larger than the couscous commonly sold. When berries are in season you can substitute the orange segments with raspberries or strawberries. This is a wonderful alternative to the more familiar rice pudding.

> 150g Israeli couscous
> juice of 2 large oranges
> 250ml water
> 125g caster sugar
> 250ml double cream
> 2 oranges, segmented

Put the couscous, orange juice, water and sugar into a saucepan and bring to the simmer. Cook like that for 25 minutes until the couscous is soft and all the liquid has been absorbed. Add more water if necessary.

When the couscous is tender, add the cream and cook for a further 5 minutes.

Just before serving add the orange segments. Serve while hot, with additional whipped cream if desired.

COST £2.80

THE WINE SELECTION

Goodness, it's all go with Silvena. I was scurrying out for nettles some weeks back; I am now invited to plunder the fields for sorrel. I did plant a sorrel patch in a garden I briefly owned 24 years ago but it grew so magnificently my next-door neighbour asked me to cut it back as it was obscuring her view of the Thames. I discovered two things from this: I didn't like living in Putney and sorrel is very difficult to pair with wine as it is deliciously bitter, disarmingly acid, and charmingly sour (as certain old wine writers care to think of themselves). Sorrel omelette, however, has had these characteristics softened and therefore I am able to recommend **Asda's Chilean Sauvignon Blanc 2002 (16 points, £2.96)**. It will work splendidly with this dish as the melon fruit with undercutting citrus will harmonise perfectly with the omelette.

For the lamb with its seemingly innocent seasonality, we also have to watch out. It is not as innocent, poor spring lamb, as it appears for it contains a complex trap (like BK2 in chess) to snare the unwary: that spicing of cumin, coriander and cardamom and its minty peas. Now my preference here, money no object, would be a robust, spicy red like **Tesco's Finest Reserve Australian Cabernet Sauvignon 2000 (16 points, £4.99)**, for it offers us tar, mint, herbs, berries and tannins all hugger-mugger, thick and rich as successful thieves. If a single bottle will do the four of you then go for it but cheaper is **Carinena Gran Tempranillo 2002 (15.5 points, £2.99, Sainsbury's)** from Spain, which has spice, texture, rich baked plums and berries with a gripping edge to its tannic finish.

For the pudding, alas, the kitty has insufficient left. However, if you're loaded, go for **Sainsbury's** own-label **Rich Cream Sherry (16.5 points, £3.99)**. Its crème brûlée and honey fruitiness will be marvellous with the couscous.

SUMMER

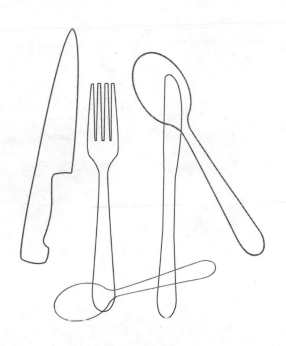

PEA SOUP with GOAT'S MILK BRIE and RYE CROÛTONS

Once Europeans ate peas only when dried in porridge. Fresh peas were an invention of the court of Louis XIV – and today they are still a luxury. Fresh peas are like small green and crunchy jewels. The season of fresh garden peas is June to August and the taste is unsurpassed. To preserve taste and colour, peas should be cooked briefly, and in the recipe below the cooking time is minimal. It is really much better to use freshly podded peas instead of frozen.

1 medium onion, finely chopped
25g butter
500g podded fresh peas
100g any greens you have available, such as spinach or lettuce
800ml chicken stock (see page 197)
salt and pepper
handful of chives

Croûtons
16 thin (3cm) rounds rye bread
60g goat's milk Brie, cut into 16 thin slices

Preheat the oven to 200°C/400°F/Gas 6. To prepare the croûtons, toast the slices of bread in the preheated oven until ready, about 5 minutes. Rye bread takes longer to toast than wheat bread, and tastes beautifully caramelised. Place a slice of Brie on each croûton and put aside.

To make the soup, sweat the onion in the butter until soft, then add the peas and greens. Pour over the stock and simmer for about 5 minutes. (You can use a good-quality vegetable stock instead.) Remove from the heat and blend in a food processor until a smooth and velvety texture is achieved. Season to taste.

To serve, ladle some of the soup into each soup dish. Arrange four Brie croûtons on top and sprinkle with chives.

COST £4.50

SCALOPPINE MARSALA

A great Italian dish! Veal is rich and elegant in flavour, and it is what the classic recipe uses. If you have reservations about using veal, then you can substitute with turkey or even chicken. Serve with fresh, springy and crunchy salad leaves.

    4 slices veal, about 100g each
    2 tbsp plain flour
    salt and pepper
    6 tbsp olive oil
    200ml Marsala or dry Madeira
    1 tsp arrowroot, mixed with 2 tsp water (optional)
    150g fresh wild mushrooms, cleaned
    handful of flat-leaf parsley, chopped

Place a veal slice on a work surface and cover with clingfilm. Pound it lightly with a meat pounder (or a heavy rolling pin) until about 1cm thick. Repeat with the rest of the meat.

Sprinkle the flour into a shallow pan. Season the scaloppine with salt and pepper, dredge in flour and shake off the excess. In a large, heavy non-stick frying pan, heat the olive oil over a medium heat. When very hot, add the veal and brown on each side, then transfer to a platter.

Add the Marsala and arrowroot (if using) to the pan and cook for about 8 minutes to just reduce it a little. Stir in the mushrooms and boil over high heat until they are tender and the liquid has reduced to about a third.

Return the veal slices to the pan, spooning the sauce over them until they are hot. Serve at once and garnish with parsley.

Cost £11.30

STRAWBERRIES ROMANOFF

This dish is a typical Russian dish, created under the influence of the French haute cuisine, imported by the Francophile nobility of St Petersburg. The Russian aristocracy used to employ French chefs, and this led to the invention of many new dishes which, although still very Russian in essence, had many French influences and flavours. Some of them were also named after prominent members of the Russian nobility – Veal Orloff and Beef Stroganoff among them. This is a very curious way of celebrating the start of the strawberry season!

200g fresh English strawberries, hulled
2 tbsp caster sugar
juice of 1 orange
100ml orange liqueur
vegetable oil for greasing
whipped double cream

Meringue
2 egg whites
1/8 tsp cream of tartar
100g caster sugar

Place the strawberries in a bowl and toss them with the sugar. Pour over them the orange juice and orange liqueur. Leave at room temperature for about 2 hours.

Meanwhile, preheat the oven to 140°C/275°F/Gas 1. Line a baking sheet with foil and grease this.

Beat the egg whites with the cream of tartar until they begin to hold soft peaks. Beat in the sugar until a thick meringue is formed.

With a spoon make four large rounds of the meringue mix on the prepared baking sheet, flattening the centres. Bake for about 1 hour. Remove to a rack to cool.

To serve, place a meringue on a dessert plate, spoon over some of the strawberries and top with some cream. Repeat with the rest of the meringues.

COST £4.10

THE WINE SELECTION

Ah! The English pea! I was paid fourpence a bag to pick peas in
Essex when I bunked off school early, and so I have a great affection
for the little green globes. They really are a most eccentric vegetable,
a striking metaphor indeed for what it is to be English: thick
skinned, private, a multiplicity of souls in an individual pod. With
Silvena's pea soup I recommend a very gently spicy white wine, and
the one which comes to mind, crisply and tangily, is **Sainsbury's**
own-label **Vin de Pays des Côtes de Gascogne (14.5 points, £3.03).** As
well as being excellent with the soup it is a very charming whistle-
wetter for the chef as she chops and slices. A glass each for the four
of you will do nicely.

The wine for the scaloppine Marsala, using chicken instead of veal
(which I would prefer thank you), is of course dependent upon a
wine of an altogether different hue and weight of fruit. How you
acquire the Marsala or Madeira on our budget I haven't a clue, but I
do know we can afford £4.98 for **two bottles** – yes, that's right,
madam, two bottles – of **Aldi's Budovar Merlot 2001 (15.5 points)**
from Hungary. This wine has a delicious screwcap and very freshly
picked berries with soft, gently brisk tannins. It will be terrific with
the scaloppine if chilled and decanted (so the wine aerates and your
guests imagine you have spent a good deal more money than in fact
you have done).

This leaves us with a whopping £1.99 to lash out on a sweet wine for
the strawberries Romanoff. I suggest we throw caution to the winds,
however, and our budget, and blue £6.99 at **Waitrose** on a bottle of
**Château Les Sablines Monbazillac 2000 (16 points, £6.99 the 50cl
bottle).** It has a waxy ripeness with honey, chalk, raspberry and
citrus. It is superb with fresh fruit as it is an immediately sensual
sweetie (not unlike Silvena, I suppose).

ROASTED BEETROOT, BLOOD ORANGE and ASPARAGUS

'Wild' asparagus is in season, a very thin and crisp version of the green asparagus with which we are so familiar. Try to use this version if you can find it. The season is so short; blink and you have missed it! Buy more and freeze it as it is in bunches. It couldn't be easier, so when the season is over you can still surprise your guests with it...

4 small beetroots, washed
12 thin green asparagus stalks, peeled
salt and pepper
100g beetroot salad leaves, washed and dried
2 small blood oranges, skinned and thinly sliced
2 tbsp shelled walnuts, lightly toasted

Walnut vinaigrette
1 tbsp red wine vinegar
1 tbsp walnut oil
2 tbsp olive oil

Preheat the oven to 180°C/350°F/Gas 4.

Trim the beetroots, wrap in foil and roast in the preheated oven for about an hour.

Cool, peel and cut each beetroot into halves or four wedges.

Cook the asparagus in boiling salted water, but very briefly, so it keeps its colour and crispy texture.

To make the walnut vinaigrette, whisk together the vinegar, walnut and olive oils. Season to taste.

Toss the beet salad leaves in the vinaigrette and place on the centre of each plate. Arrange the beetroot, asparagus and blood orange slices on top. Sprinkle with walnuts.

COST £3.20

PORK BELLY stuffed with ROASTED GARLIC and MUSHROOMS

Pork belly is rich and succulent, a very much overlooked and underrated cut. Ask your butcher to cut from the thicker end of the belly as it is for stuffing, and make sure you get the best possible quality meat. The belly has so much more flavour than the regular Sunday roast joints. Serve the meat in its own juices.

    2 bulbs spring garlic
    150g wild mushrooms, cleaned
    1 shallot, finely chopped
    15g butter
    5 tbsp finely chopped parsley
    200g minced pork
    salt and pepper
    800g pork belly

Preheat the oven to 200°C/400°F/Gas 6.

Wrap the garlic in foil and roast in the oven for about 45 minutes. When ready, remove from the foil and allow to cool. Cut just the top of each bulb of garlic and squeeze the soft garlic paste out into a dish.

In a frying pan, cook the mushrooms and shallot in the butter until tender. Finely chop them and place in a large bowl with the roasted garlic, parsley, minced pork and salt and pepper to taste. Mix well.

To prepare the pork belly, place the belly on a board and insert a long, very sharp knife through the side of the cut end of the belly, creating a pocket that goes through to the other side. You can ask your butcher to do this for you. Fill the belly with the mushroom mixture.

Fry the pork belly in a very hot pan on a medium heat for about 12 minutes until golden brown. Roast the pork belly in the oven for about 45–60 minutes.

Serve hot, cut into thick pieces accompanied by its cooking juices, with new season Jersey Royal potatoes.

COST £11.45

PECAN and WHITE CHOCOLATE SEMIFREDDO

Semifreddo is a wonderfully quick dessert. You can easily prepare it on the morning of your party and have it ready for the evening. Like pannacotta, it is cream based and you can add your own flavours to it. Instead of pecans, feel free to use hazelnuts or walnuts.

> 100g caster sugar
> 60g shelled pecan nuts, chopped
> 2 eggs
> 60g white chocolate, broken into pieces
> 300ml double cream, whipped

Place half of the sugar in a heavy-bottomed saucepan and let it caramelise over a medium heat. You need to be very vigilant when cooking the sugar as it may burn and become very bitter. Once the sugar has caramelised it should be very lightly brown in colour and of a thick sauce consistency. Add the chopped pecans and cook for just a minute. While hot, pour the mixture on to a cold surface, preferably a marble or granite slab if you have one, and allow to cool and become very hard. At this stage finely chop the 'croccante' and keep to one side.

Whip the eggs and remaining sugar together in a bowl until very pale and creamy, and place on top of a pan of simmering water. Keep whisking until the mixture becomes thick in consistency, then remove from the bain-marie to cool.

Now melt the chocolate in another bowl over simmering water. When it has cooled a little, add to the egg mixture, together with the whipped cream and the chopped croccante.

Pour into individual small pots and freeze for 2 hours before serving.

COST £4.80

THE WINE SELECTION

I sometimes wonder from where Silvena gets her ideas. Does some kind of culinary succubus visit her in the dead of night? Did she discover these outrageous recipes at her mother's elbow? Does everyone eat like this in Bulgaria? (As if it were not obvious to readers by now, my dear colleague is a Bulgar.) And I, of course, am the Vulgar. I have to find demotic liquids under a tenner to go with these devious luxury goods and frankly, contemplating my primary dish of beetroot, blood orange and asparagus, I struggle. But in my distress a blessed succubus visits me (!) and it whispers TESCO! Thus with one bound I am free and with that preposterously delicious first course I find the non-vintage, own-label **Tesco Chilean White (16 points, £2.97)**! It offers chewy gooseberry fruit with a hint of calomine.

And with that wickedly stuffed pork? I cross the aisle and reach for two bottles of **Tesco Chilean Red (15 points, £2.99)** which is juicy, as it needs to be with this dish, but dry, offering a hint of tobacco to its under-ripe cherries. Both these terrific bargains are screwcapped so the fruit will stay fresh and feisty for months.

This leaves us with £1.05p in our purse for a dessert wine and though you can, as advised elsewhere, consider it already spent on the **16-point**, under **£3.99** bottle of **Sainsbury's** (or **Tesco's**) deliciously honied **Moscatel de Valencia**, it is possible, for those with an urge to be a little more adventurous in seeking the perfect partner for that pecan and white chocolate pud, to plunder the same **Tesco** wine aisles for a half bottle of **Muscat de Beaumes de Venise (16 points, £4.49)**. This golden liquid is suggestive of ripe pineapple with honey and a touch of toffee apple. A small glass each will finish you off nicely.

TABBOULEH SALAD with GRAPES and PISTACHIO NUTS
PAN-FRIED FILLET of TUNA with GAZPACHO SAUCE
ROASTED VANILLA PEACHES served on TOASTED BRIOCHE

TABBOULEH SALAD with GRAPES and PISTACHIO NUTS

This is a very light and fluffy tabbouleh salad with fresh grapes and lightly toasted pistachio nuts. I have added sweet, juicy and ripe tomatoes, crunchy green pepper and zesty lemon, which give the salad a gazpacho-like taste and texture.

200g bulgur wheat
2 large ripe tomatoes, finely diced
1/2 green pepper, seeded and chopped
1/2 cucumber, peeled and finely sliced
80g white seedless grapes, halved
1 small garlic clove, crushed
salt and pepper
40ml olive oil
juice of 1 lemon
5 tbsp chopped parsley
3 tbsp chopped mint
3 tbsp shelled pistachios, lightly toasted

Cook the bulgur wheat in plenty of hot water until soft, about 15 minutes. Drain well and keep aside.

In a large bowl mix together the tomatoes, green pepper, cucumber, grapes and garlic. Add the bulgur wheat and mix well. Season with salt and pepper, then add the olive oil and lemon juice, and finally mix in the parsley and mint.

Let the salad stand in the fridge for about 2 hours. Sprinkle with pistachio nuts just before serving.

Cost £2.60

PAN-FRIED FILLET of TUNA with GAZPACHO SAUCE

A perfect dish for a hot summer's day, when you want something fresh and healthy but with the least effort. This has a wonderful sweet and sour taste that appeals when the weather is hot. You can replace the tuna with white fish such as cod, or even with chicken or turkey fillet.

4 x 150g tuna fillets
2 tbsp olive oil
salt and pepper
200g fresh salad leaves, washed and dried
2 tbsp olive oil
2 tbsp balsamic vinegar

Gazpacho sauce
3 vine-ripened tomatoes, cored, seeded and finely chopped
1/2 cucumber, peeled and finely diced
1/2 each of red and green pepper, seeded and finely chopped
1 garlic clove, crushed
2 tbsp black olives, pitted and chopped
3 tbsp olive oil
1 tbsp balsamic vinegar
4 tbsp chopped coriander
3 tbsp basil leaves

To make the sauce, mix all the sauce ingredients together and keep in the fridge until ready to use. I have substituted coriander for the parsley so typical of the conventional gazpacho sauce.

To cook the tuna, heat the olive oil in a heavy sauté pan and pan-fry the fillets for about 3–6 minutes on each side, depending on how well done you like your tuna. Season to taste.

Place the tuna fillets on to a serving plate and spoon some gazpacho sauce over them. In a separate small bowl, dress the salad leaves with the olive oil, balsamic vinegar and salt and pepper to taste. Serve some leaves to the side of the tuna.

COST £12.80

ROASTED VANILLA PEACHES served on TOASTED BRIOCHE

The combination of roasted fruit and toasted cake is not a new, trendy concept, but has been around for a while. Using fresh seasonal peaches is very satisfying and easy, and vanilla-roasted peaches are truly delicious. After all, vanilla is the world's favourite flavour and, with its feel-good-factor qualities, is perfect when used in desserts. Do not settle for bottled substitutes, but use a real vanilla pod.

4 medium peaches, halved and stoned
1 vanilla pod
40ml water
60g caster sugar
4 brioche slices, toasted
100g mascarpone cheese
1 tbsp icing sugar

Preheat the oven to 200°C/400°F/Gas 6. In a shallow baking tray, place the peach halves cut-sides up.

Split the vanilla pod and scrape the seeds into a small saucepan. Add the split pod, the water and sugar and bring to the boil. Simmer until the sugar has dissolved and the vanilla has began to infuse.

Pour this syrup over the peaches and place in the preheated oven to bake for 20 minutes, until the peaches are soft and beginning to brown.

To serve, place a toasted brioche slice on a serving plate and top with two peach halves. Drizzle over some vanilla sauce and accompany with a dollop of mascarpone. Dust with some icing sugar.

COST £4.40

THE WINE SELECTION

Is it possible to find a wine which could go through a whole menu
unaided? This does not depend so much on the wine as on the
courses and such is Silvena's wily dexterity and breadth of palate-
pounding inventiveness that rarely – indeed never until now – has
she ever composed a menu where one could, and I emphasise *could*,
just about, and I emphasise *just about*, find a wine which might
possibly, and I emphasise *might possibly*, carry us through this whole
menu encompassing on the way tabbouleh salad (watching out for
the mint), tuna with gazpacho sauce (noting the basil, coriander and
balsamic vinegar), and those roasted peaches (with their clever,
devilish addition of vanilla). Uniquely, there is one wine region in the
world where such a wine is grown and raised, vinified and matured.
It is the Loire. It is the Chenin Blanc grape which features and it
comes packaged as Vouvray Demi-Sec (this latter designation often
being an off-putting misnomer as such is the superb balancing
acidity in good specimens of this wine that it is no more sweet on
the palate than the average Aussie Chardonnay – but it is far more
versatile, long-lasting and decisive with myriad dishes). Now every
few years or so I buy, from my local Sainsbury's, Vouvray La
Couronne des Plantagenets Chapelle de Cray. I wait until it is
reduced, as it always is. It ends up, the last lot I bought, around
£3.50 a bottle (maybe less). I am currently drinking at home the
1996, bought at least five or six years ago, and it needs this long to
mature into something interesting and combative. The current
vintage is 2002 (costing, undiscounted, £4.99). It is superior to my
'96 or rather will become so in four or five years, and I suggest you
get hold of some in the next Sainsbury's sale and stick the bottles
away somewhere dark and cool, lying them on their side as they are
not yet screwcapped and still have old-fashioned corks. Does this
mean you will have to wait half-a-decade to prepare this menu? Have
pity, you cry, and pity I concede you. A visit to **Tesco** is now required

for **Vouvray Demi-Sec Gaston Dorleans 2002 (16 points** now, 18.5
points in four to eight years, £5.99). This finely textured Chenin
Blanc has tangy pineapple, a hint of mango, a touch of citrus. It is
more immediately capable of handling this menu than the Chapelle
de Cray but, as with that wine, cellaring Gaston Dorleans will
concentrate the fruit, deepen the acids, increase the aroma; it will
broaden the wine. Its maker, Fred Bourillon, has worked on the
Gaston Dorleans cuvées for Tesco for a decade now (in addition to
the 50 acres of his own vines). This involves eight vineyard-owning
neighbours, with mature vines (average age 27 years), whom
Monsieur Bourillon oversees. This allows Tesco to buy an unusually
large amount of the same wine and for its consistency to be
maintained. Fermentation of all the grapes takes place in the
Bourillon winery under the tufa cliffs that dominate the small village
of Rochecourbon, just down the road from Vouvray. Fermentation
depends on natural yeasts and is temperature controlled. The ageing
on the lees, the bits and bobs left over from the wine-making, lasts
three months with 95% of the wine in stainless steel, the other 5%
being kept in already used, one-year-old barrels. The resultant blend,
in the case of the 2002, achieves a profusely Loire white wine but
one which surely deserves more universal appeal. To my palate and
pocket, it represents a stunning bargain – again just like the
Chapelle de Cray. Et voilà! – we have our wine to take us through this
menu (though it will feel a little bruised up against those peaches
and so sips of water won't go amiss between mouthfuls).

RUSSIAN or OLIVIER SALAD

Menu 4

CHICKEN with GRAPES and APRICOTS

CHERRY STRUDEL

RUSSIAN or OLIVIER SALAD

This Russian salad is typical, it seems, not only of Russia but of many hotel and restaurant menus in western Europe as well. It comes by the same name but in many different forms, and you can easily be put off if you've had one that was badly prepared. Olivier – the French chef of Czar Nicholas II – created the salad in around 1860. A home-made mayonnaise is essential (and the recipe here will make more than you need).

> 200g piece of cooked ham, diced
> 1 large potato, boiled, peeled and diced
> 1 large carrot, boiled, peeled and diced
> 100g cooked peas
> 2 medium gherkins, diced
> 2 eggs, hard-boiled and diced
> 50g freshly cooked green beans, chopped
> 1/2 tbsp Dijon mustard
> salt and pepper
> 2 tbsp chopped parsley
>
> *Home-made mayonnaise*
> 1 egg
> 1 hard-boiled egg yolk
> 150ml olive oil
> 2 tbsp lemon juice

To prepare the home-made mayonnaise, you will need a food processor. Combine the raw egg and cooked egg yolk, season with salt and pepper and blend well. With the motor running, start to add a fine stream of olive oil. Here you need patience, as you need to add the oil very slowly. If you are too quick, the consistency will be more like a sauce than a thick creamy mayonnaise. Add the lemon juice and keep until needed in the fridge.

In a large bowl mix the ham, potato, carrot, peas, gherkins, eggs, beans and mustard, and season to taste. Add about 4 tbsp mayonnaise and mix, making sure that you don't crush the vegetables too much. Add the parsley and serve.

COST £4.40

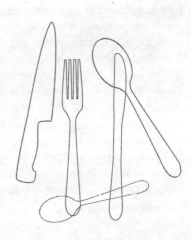

CHICKEN with GRAPES and APRICOTS

There are many versions of this recipe and the one below, with Turkish and slight Bulgarian origins, is prepared with fresh fruits rather than dried. It works well with dried fruits as well, though, which can be used in the recipe in the winter. Please note that the chicken has to be marinated, so you need to start preparations the day before.

    1 tbsp runny honey
    1 tsp grated fresh root ginger
    1 tsp ground cinnamon
    1 tsp freshly ground black pepper
    100ml white wine
    1 large chicken, about 1.8kg, quartered
    3 tbsp olive oil
    1 onion, chopped
    300ml water
    1 cinnamon stick
    100g seedless grapes, halved
    100g fresh apricots, halved and stoned
    2 tbsp black sesame seeds, toasted

In a large bowl combine the honey, ginger, cinnamon, pepper and wine, and stir together. Rub the mix over the chicken and let it marinate in the fridge overnight, covered.

Heat the olive oil in a large sauté pan, and sauté the onion until just golden in colour. Add the drained chicken and brown all the pieces evenly, turning them around. Now add the chicken marinade, water and cinnamon stick, and simmer for 30 minutes. By this point the liquid should have reduced by about half, and the chicken pieces should be cooked.

Finally add the grapes and apricot halves and simmer for 5–8 minutes further. Serve almost immediately, sprinkled with the sesame seeds, accompanied by plain boiled rice.

COST £ 10.20

CHERRY STRUDEL

A true strudel should be fine, crisp and light, with very thin pastry filled with fruit. Apple is the most common filling in a strudel, but cherries, especially when they are in season, make this dessert a real luxury.

60g butter, melted, plus extra for greasing
2 tbsp cherry jam
500g fresh cherries, stoned
70g shelled pecan nuts, roughly chopped
80g caster sugar, plus extra for sprinkling
30g brioche breadcrumbs
10 large sheets fresh filo pastry
icing sugar to decorate

Preheat the oven to 200°C/400°F/Gas 6. Butter and line a flat baking tray. In a small saucepan place the cherry jam and heat slowly until just melted.

In a bowl mix the cherries, nuts, sugar and breadcrumbs. On the working surface in front of you lay out a damp cloth and place a sheet of filo pastry on it. Brush generously with melted butter, then cover with another sheet of filo, brushing again with butter. Repeat the same process with the rest of the sheets, brushing with the melted cherry jam every now and again as well as the butter. You can do that on every third filo sheet.

Once you have all the filo buttered and stacked in front of you, place the cherry and pecan mixture in the middle of it and roll the pastry up as though it were a Swiss roll.

Butter the roll on all sides, sprinkle on some extra caster sugar and curl into a horseshoe shape. Place on the prepared tray and bake in the preheated oven for 20–30 minutes, until golden brown.

Dust with icing sugar when cool, and serve warm or cold.

COST £4.20

THE WINE SELECTION

Be thankful. I am not going to recommend a Russian wine for that salad starter. I did once drink a Georgian wine – about as close as I ever got to a Russian one. It was the worst red wine I had ever drunk (up until 1998 when a Cretan red retsina took over the top spot for yukky vinous liquids), and I recommended it to a bloke who tried to take out my then girlfriend. I do not know if he died of shock, but he certainly disappeared from the picture. The other mystery is in the name of this menu's starter. Silvena may be right that the dish is named after Czar Nicholas's chef but I was told – admittedly by a drunken actor – that Larry Olivier, that once-towering forever-knightly thespian presence, created this salad whilst on the set of *The Prince and the Showgirl* with Marilyn Monroe. I think I was lied to, don't you? Ms Monroe would have understood. Ah well, let us turn to the wine to go with it which needs to be a white because of the acidity in the mustard dressing. I cannot think of a single red which would go with Olivier salad and so we must go a Chilean Sauvignon Blanc, Aussie Sémillon, New Zealand Riesling or Sauvignon Blanc, or a German Kabinett from the Moselle or the Rhine (also the Pfalz if the grape is a Pinot Gris). Indeed, it is the last-named wine region we must visit and plunder and bring back with us **Villa Wolf Pinot Gris 2001** (16.5 points, £5.99, **Sainsbury's**). It shows gorgeous demure citrus, nuts and apricot with a concentrated yet delicate texture. It is very classy, very delicious. Failing this, there is the much more widely distributed **Kendermanns Pinot Grigio 2002**, also from the **Pfalz** (16 points, £4.03), and this is lean, crisp and very refreshing (and deeply mayonnaise-tolerant).

Tolerance, however, is not exactly the word which comes to mind when we consider that chicken. Not just chicken, Silvena, but chicken with grapes and apricots! Oh dear, my dear, you don't make it easy for me, do you? And you add honey, fresh ginger and cinnamon. The wine which occurs to me as its natural partner is one of those rich, slightly bitter-sweet Italian reds from Verona. An Amarone della Valpolicella Classico to be exact. Here semi-dried red grapes are used to concentrate the flavours and they will transport that chicken to heaven, and us along with it if we're prepared to shell out the necessary dosh, for we are not talking cheap here. The Wine Society has such a wine, a 1998, costing £26 but you have to be a member to buy there. **Oddbins**, however, merely require you to be a member of the human race (proven by waving a credit card at the cash till) and so we can do business instantly. I suggest you consider **Masi Amarone della Valpolicella 1999 (£19.99)**, **Masi Recioto della Valpolicella 1999 (£19.99)**, **Musella Amarone della Valpolicella (£22.49)** and **Funellin Amarone della Valpolicella San Antonio 1998 (£34.99)**. Budget? Oh, go to hell.

And whilst you're about it, take that cherry strudel with you. It is disgustingly delicious and utterly wicked and will suit hell very nicely. The wine to go with you (and it)? Take the wine I recommend for the pud in the Winter menu 3, namely **Oddbins' Maculan Dindarello (£6.99** the half bottle). It is also Italian and whilst not hellishly expensive is certainly devilishly gorgeous on the tongue (even the forked variety set within a hornèd head).

PECORINO and PINE NUT STUFFED TOMATOES

While tomatoes are at their best, try stuffing them with a delicious mixture of Camargue rice, pecorino cheese and pine nuts. This could be prepared earlier in the day and then just cooked in the oven before serving. Pecorino is an Italian hard cheese available in good supermarkets and delis.

8 medium ripe tomatoes
40g butter
1 onion, chopped
200g Camargue rice
80g pine nuts
100g pecorino cheese, freshly grated
2 tbsp chopped parsley
salt and pepper

Preheat the oven to 180°C/350°F/Gas 4.

To prepare the tomatoes, cut a lid from each one and remove the seeds and pulp. Scrape all of it from the inside of the tomatoes, making sure that there isn't any left in. Keep the pulp and seeds. Arrange the tomatoes in a shallow baking dish.

Melt the butter in a medium saucepan, cook the onion until soft, then add the tomato pulp and seeds. Meanwhile cook the rice in boiling water for about 12 minutes or until semi-cooked. Drain and add to the onion and tomato, with the pine nuts, cheese and parsley. Season well with salt and pepper, and stir well.

Fill the tomatoes with the mixture, and replace the lids on each tomato. Place in the hot oven and bake for about 30 minutes. Serve hot as a starter, as here, or cold as a snack.

Cost £4.20

MONKFISH PLAKI

'Plaki' is a Greek and Bulgarian method of baking fish. It is the perfect summer fish dish, cooked with a lot of wonderful, seasonal vegetables. You can prepare plaki with other kinds of fish, like cod or sea bass.

600g monkfish tail, boned
2 onions, chopped
3 garlic cloves, chopped
6 tbsp olive oil
300g fresh plum tomatoes, chopped
100ml dry white wine
100ml water
100g green olives
100g spinach, washed and chopped
salt and pepper
60g shelled walnuts, coarsely chopped
200g plain white basmati rice
5 tbsp each of chopped parsley and basil

Preheat the oven to 180°C/350°F/Gas 4. Remove the middle bone from the monkfish and any membrane or skin, if you haven't asked the fishmonger to do that for you already. Cut the monkfish fillet into small 2cm pieces.

Sauté the onion and garlic in the oil in a heavy, deep casserole until soft and golden. Make sure that they don't brown too much. Add the tomatoes, wine and water, bring to the boil, and after 3 minutes simmer for a further 10 minutes. The cooking liquid will be slightly reduced by this point.

Stir in the whole olives and spinach, then arrange the monkfish pieces on top. Season and let simmer for about 8 minutes. Add the walnuts. Cover the casserole, transfer to the preheated oven, and cook for a further 15 minutes.

Meanwhile boil the rice in salted water until cooked, then drain well. Serve the monkfish plaki with the rice, sprinkled with the herbs.

COST £10.30

SIMPLE CHOCOLATE and ORANGE CUSTARD

Orange and chocolate are natural partners, the flavours of both blending perfectly. The elegant citrus of the orange cuts the richness of the chocolate allowing us at the same time to still enjoy the velvety and rich experience of the chocolate. Use really good-quality chocolate for this simple recipe.

    4 oranges, washed
    2 tbsp caster sugar
    6 egg yolks
    460ml double cream
    130g milk chocolate, chopped

Finely grate the zest from all four oranges, then cut off the peel and divide the oranges into segments. Keep aside.

To make the custard, whisk the sugar and egg yolks in a double boiler over just simmering water for 10 minutes, until volumised and thickened.

Mix the cream and the orange zest and bring to the boil. Pour over the chocolate in a bowl, and stir until the chocolate has melted. Add the chocolate to the egg and sugar mixture, and cook gently in the double boiler until the custard has thickened.

Pour the chocolate and orange custard into a large, shallow glass dish, and place in the refrigerator to set.

To serve, spoon some of the custard into individual serving plates, and garnish with orange segments.

COST £3.80

THE WINE SELECTION

Well, baking those stuffed tomatoes softens the acids and makes them far less intimidating for any wine. Hmm. This requires more thought than you might think (if you'll pardon the term). Let us leave the dish for a moment and consider the monkfish. Hmm. Tomatoes here, too. And spinach. Now my hesitation here is because tomatoes have great integrity and change less, on the palate, than many other fruits when not over-cooked; though, as I say, roasting, baking and frying does significantly alter the acid structure and provide a softer, perhaps charred feel. I am hesitant because, frankly, I can swing both ways with both of these dishes. There are red and white wines which will both work. It all depends on your preferences. I'm also minded to find a wine which will equally enhance both dishes, not just one at the expense of the other. Within my budget, then, I'm going to suggest **Waitrose's Trincaria Sicilia Bianco 2002 (16.5 points, £2.99)**, a delicious 50–50 blend of local Inzolia and Catarratto grapes. It has gorgeously smoky, slightly charred gooseberry and pear fruit with demure citrus. It is a soft yet dry wine of great class (and for the money a miracle). Three bottles of this will see you safely past the stuffed toms (it'll feel utterly at home with the pecorino), and with the monkfish plaki it'll be a doddle. If a red appeals more to your taste, then no problem (as long as it is lightly chilled). I suggest **Beaumes de Venise, Côtes du Rhône-Villages 2001 (17.5 points, £5.79, at selected Somerfield** stores). Goodness me, what a wonderful red wine for the money this is. It has superb berries, spice, texture and a smoky finish of delicacy and precision. It is finely balanced, has coffee-edged tannins and a finish to make the eyebrows shoot up and the socks to fly. Two bottles of it take you over budget but, well, what's £1.58 when all's said and done?

I'd like the wine for the dessert to come cheap, too, but the zestiness of those oranges and the richness of the chocolate do deem it necessary for a complex wine to be the order of the day and **Waitrose** has **Maury Vin Doux Naturel** at 16.5% alcohol in the half bottle for £3.99 or £95.76 the 24-bottle case delivered through **Waitrose Direct**.

SUMMER GREENS SALAD with ROQUEFORT VINAIGRETTE

This is a very simple, yet wonderful mixture of seasonal salad leaves, perfect for a summer evening. Use whatever is fresh on the market – radicchio, endive, lamb's lettuce, dandelion leaves – and any herbs you may wish to add, such as chervil, mint or parsley. The velvety and creamy vinaigrette sits luxuriously upon the fresh, crisp and transparent salad leaves. It is very much what makes this salad exciting and interesting.

> 200g mixed salad leaves, washed, dried and torn into bite-sized
>   pieces
> handful each of chervil, mint and parsley
> handful of sultanas
> salt and pepper ·
>
> *Roquefort vinaigrette*
> juice of 1 lemon
> 120ml grapeseed oil
> 120g best-quality Roquefort cheese, crumbled

Place the greens and herbs in a large salad bowl.

To prepare the vinaigrette, combine the lemon juice, grapeseed oil and cheese. Blend well. Toss the salad leaves with the vinaigrette and finally sprinkle with the sultanas. Season to taste.

Cost £4.20

JUNIPER FILLET of DUCK with RHUBARB CHUTNEY

A very rich and fruity main course with some spice and sweetness! I have chosen duck but you can substitute pork. The rhubarb chutney can be stored in the fridge for at least two weeks. The chutney is also good with plain risotto or with cheese sandwiches. Serve with boiled new or, best, Jersey Royal potatoes.

4 medium duck breasts
1 tbsp juniper berries, finely crushed
½ tsp each of sea salt and cracked black pepper
2 tbsp olive oil
25ml port
500g new or Jersey potatoes, scrubbed and washed
mint sprigs

Rhubarb chutney
2 tsp golden sultanas
1 shallot, finely chopped
25g caster sugar
2 tbsp white wine vinegar
½ cinnamon stick
½ tsp freshly grated nutmeg
200g rhubarb, washed and cut into small pieces

Preheat the oven to 180°C/350°F/Gas 4.

Put the duck on a plate in one layer. Mix the juniper berries, sea salt and cracked black pepper together, then rub the duck with half the olive oil and all the juniper mixture. Let it stand in the fridge for about 2 hours.

Heat the remaining oil in a heavy sauté pan and brown the duck on all sides. Now place in an oven dish and roast in the preheated oven for about 20 minutes, or longer if you like your duck well done. During cooking, baste with the port. When ready, remove the duck from the pan and rest in a warm place before slicing.

Boil the potatoes with some salt and the mint. Keep warm until ready to serve.

For the rhubarb chutney, place the sultanas, shallot, sugar, vinegar and spices in a small saucepan and stir and simmer for 5–6 minutes. Add the rhubarb and cover, then simmer on the same low heat for 5 more minutes or until soft. Remove the cinnamon stick.

Serve the duck sliced, accompanied by the new potatoes and a spoonful of the rhubarb chutney.

COST £9.80

COCONUT PANNACOTTA, served with PALM SUGAR and BAILEY'S SYRUP

This is a variation of the classic pannacotta, which is prepared with cream only. Coconut cream is not the easiest to work with in desserts, as it has a different fat content from that of cream. This recipe serves six people, or the four of the rest of the menu, with two of you being greedy!

    3 gelatine leaves
    750ml double cream
    100ml coconut cream
    220g caster sugar
    200g brown palm sugar, grated
    100ml water
    60ml Bailey's Irish Cream

Soften the gelatine in cold water and then wring out the excess water.

Place the double cream, coconut cream and half of the caster sugar in a saucepan and heat gently to boiling point, stirring occasionally. Add the gelatine and stir until dissolved.

Pour the liquid into six ramekin dishes and after they have cooled, place in the fridge to set for at least 12 hours.

Meanwhile place the palm sugar, remaining caster sugar and water in a saucepan and cook until it forms a syrup. Add the Bailey's, and cool.

Serve the cold coconut pannacotta with its palm sugar and Bailey's syrup.

COST £4.20

THE WINE SELECTION

A salad of summer greens with a vinaigrette of Roquefort is a wonderful way to start a meal. Blue cheese as tangy as Roquefort, however, is a potent force albeit softened and mollified by other ingredients (and the addition of the sultanas presents a further tricky hurdle for any wine to negotiate). My immediate reaction, therefore, is to go down to the cellar and bring back a bottle of ancient German Riesling of Spätlese ripeness (that is to say a wine with a sweetish edge made from late-picked grapes). My budget, though, will not stretch to this beauteous accompaniment but it will, thanks to **Morrison's** supermarkets, certainly stretch to this retailer's **Zimmermann Riesling, Pfalz 2002 (16 points, £2.99)** which offers sprightly ripe melon with a hint of honey and crisp compensating acids. It will do the dish proud and also set up the palate nicely for that equally demanding juniper duck fillet with its wicked rhubarb chutney (stroke of genius that, Silvena, my girl). Now my instinct here is also for a rich white wine and a return to the cellar to find some Alsatian Tokay-Pinot Gris but my purse cannot cope with such luxuries and so I must stick with **Morrison's** and acquire two bottles of **Falcon Ridge Chardonnay 2001 (15.5 points, £2.99)**. This is a Vin de Pays d'Oc in the modern manner (note the ingratiatingly Anglophone name of this wine) and it provides firm gooseberry and melon fruit, a sprinkling of citrus, and a vague suggestion of something toasted and nutty as it finishes.

This leaves me with £1.03p for a wine to go with that miraculous coconut pannacotta. This staggeringly delicious pudding really does demand we go mad and so we must nip along the street to **Aldi** and blue £3.29 on a bottle of **Fletchers Cream Sherry (16 points)** with its remarkable undertone of toffee and crème brûlée.

GRILSE MARINATED with BEETROOT and ORANGE

Regular readers of my column will have noticed that beetroot is one my favourite foods. Here beetroot is used in combination with orange in a marinade for grilse, a small wild salmon that is only in season for a short time. Grilse is my preferred option, but you can also use sea trout or wild salmon. Expect to pay about £6–8 per kilo for grilse. This is a really spectacular looking dish.

1 x 500g piece grilse fillet, scaled, bones removed
3 tbsp Maldon salt
4 tbsp granulated sugar
300g raw beetroot, peeled and finely grated
finely grated zest of 2 oranges
½ small bunch each of dill, chervil, parsley and basil, all finely chopped

To garnish
handful of curly endive heart
4 radishes, shredded
handful of parsley leaves

Place the grilse on a chopping board with the skin facing down.

Mix the salt, sugar, beetroot, orange zest and mixed herbs together. Now press the mixture over the top of the salmon. Wrap with clingfilm and place a heavy tray on top of the grilse fillet. Weigh down and chill for 24 hours.

After 24 hours, unwrap the fish and remove some of the coating ingredients. Rinse the grilse under cold running water. Pat dry with kitchen paper and wrap in clingfilm. Keep chilled until ready to serve.

To serve, slice very thin slices of the marinated grilse and arrange in the centre of a serving plate. Garnish with endive hearts, radish and parsley leaves.

Cost £6.80

FENNEL-CRUSTED QUAIL with CORIANDER GREMOLATA

A most unusual and quick meal. In order that both legs and breasts cook evenly, butterfly the quail, by cutting out the backbone, opening the quail up and pressing it down flat. The crushed fennel and coriander seeds form an aromatic crust when the quails are browned in the hot pan.

1–1½ tbsp fennel seeds
1 tsp coriander seeds
½ tsp rock salt
½ tsp coarsely ground black pepper
4 quails, about 125g each, cleaned
4 tbsp olive oil
150g fresh green salad leaves, washed and dried
juice of 1 lemon

Gremolata
1 tsp minced garlic
½ tsp salt
3 tsp finely grated lemon zest
small bunch of coriander, finely chopped
2 tsp olive oil

Roast the fennel and coriander seeds in a heavy pan over a moderate heat until fragrant. Transfer to a spice grinder and coarsely grind them. Stir in the salt and pepper.

To prepare the quail, place each quail, breast down, on a work surface. Cut down the backbone and remove it. Open the quail out, turn it over, and press down with the palm of your hand to flatten it. Press the quail breast down on to the fennel mixture until completely coated, sprinkling the sides as well.

To make the gremolata, mix the minced garlic, salt and lemon zest together. Add the coriander and oil and mix well. Set aside.

Heat a large non-stick pan or cast-iron grill over a medium to high heat. Add half the oil and cook the quail one by one by placing them, skin-side down, on to the hot surface. Cook for about 5 minutes or until the skin is crisp. Turn the quail over and cook for 5 more minutes. The breast of the quail should be medium rare and feel springy when touched.

To serve, place a quail on each dinner plate and sprinkle with gremolata. Serve with the crisp green salad leaves tossed in the remaining olive oil and the lemon juice.

COST £9.50

PINK PEPPERCORN MERINGUES with BERRIES

These delicate pink peppercorn meringues are delightfully crisp, with a barely sharp flavour – but not so strong that it overpowers the berries.

    5 egg whites
    300g caster sugar
    2 tsp cornflour
    1 tsp white wine vinegar
    2 tbsp pink peppercorns
    300ml double cream, whipped
    a bowl of freshly picked berries

Preheat the oven to 180°C/350°F/Gas 4. Lightly oil a large flat tray and line it with non-stick baking paper.

Beat the egg whites until thick with shiny peaks. Beat in the sugar a little at a time, then beat in the cornflour and vinegar. Do not over-mix. Make four to six large meringues by scooping dollops of the egg white on to the lined tray. Don't worry about them looking uniformly shaped.

Crush the pink peppercorns and rub most of them through a sieve over the individual meringues. Place the meringue tray in the preheated oven and immediately turn the temperature down to 150°C/300°F/Gas 2. Cook the meringues for about 50 minutes without opening the door. When cooked they should be a pale honey colour. Turn off the oven and let the meringues cool completely before removing them.

To serve, place a meringue on to a dessert plate, spoon on some cream and top with berries. Rub the remaining peppercorns through a sieve on top of the cream and berries.

COST £3.20

THE WINE SELECTION

'Grilse for supper, darlings!' doesn't sound like it'll set anyone's heart racing until you add the essential magic ingredient, 'It's one of Silvena's recipes.' Your guests will then drool over the dish which its cunning marinade of beetroot and orange has turned into a sort of colourful gravad-grilse. It must also be noted that radish accompanies the finished dish which adds to the lustre but makes the wine-waiter-on-budget's job even trickier. The perfect wine for this dish is **Villa Wolf Pinot Gris 2001 (16.5 points, £5.99, Sainsbury's)** from Germany which offers gorgeous citrus, nuts and apricot fruit. But on my budget I must look elsewhere and so may I propose **Tesco's** non-vintage **Argentinian White** in the 3-litre wine box **(16 points, £11.49)**? This offers saucy grapefruit and dry honey fruit and of course you won't drink it all, merely a third (keeping the rest for future recipes), and so we've spent £3.83 on sufficient wine for four people for the first course.

So we can afford to go barmy with the wine for the quail. Quail? Did I say quail? Silly me. This is Silvena, remember, and nothing so simple as mere quail is on offer, but a far more complex fennel-crusted quail with coriander gremolata. The wine to suit it gloriously is **Marks & Spencer's Clos Roques d'Aspes Faugères Cave de Lauren 2000 (17 points, £6.99)**. This red offers stunning mouth-filling blackberries and raspberries with the thorns included (chocolate coated) so it has the character to mix it with those wicked little spices.

This leaves me penniless for any wine to go with the meringues. Unless, that is, you want to fork out for **Sainsbury's** unctuously honied **16-point Domaine Leonce Cuisset Saussignac 2001**. It will advance the deliciousness of the dessert but it will set you back £6.99.

SLOW-ROASTED TOMATOES with GOLDEN SULTANAS

One of the biggest pleasures of summer is the abundance of ripe, sweet-tasting tomatoes. Stewed, roasted, stuffed, preserved or just eaten raw, tomatoes are utterly delicious.

> 8 plum tomatoes, halved, or 300g vine cherry tomatoes
> 4 garlic cloves, thinly sliced
> 4 shallots, finely chopped
> bunch of basil, leaves only
> 10g brown sugar
> 1/2 tsp ground cinnamon
> salt and pepper
> 50ml olive oil
> 50g plump and juicy golden sultanas

Preheat the oven to 150°C/300°F/Gas 2.

Place the halved plum or whole cherry tomatoes in a shallow roasting dish. Mix the garlic, shallots, basil, sugar, cinnamon and salt and pepper. Scatter the mixture over the tomatoes and sprinkle the olive oil on top. Place in the oven and immediately reduce the heat to 140C°/275°F/Gas 1. Roast for about 1 hour.

Scatter the golden sultanas on top, and leave in the oven for a further 30 minutes or until the tomatoes are soft and slightly caramelised. Serve warm or cold with crusty bread.

COST £2.20

ROASTED FILLET of JOHN DORY on CAVOLO NERO and MASCARPONE POTATO CAKE

John Dory, sometimes referred to as 'St Peter's fish', is never landed in any great quantity. Its appearance is rather off-putting, but do not be deceived, for John Dory is by far one of the finest fish you will ever eat. By late summer, West Country John Dory should have begun to appear, and its normally high price should be a bit more reasonable.

The bones are amongst the best for stock, so save them! John Dory is cooked simply and delicately. Cavolo nero, with its distinctive flavour, is a wonderful alternative to spinach, and is in season too.

4 x 150g fillets John Dory, skinned
80g butter, melted
salt and pepper
basil leaves and extra virgin olive oil for garnish

Potato cakes
100g cavolo nero, washed
300g cooked mashed potato
80g mascarpone cheese
50g Parmesan, freshly grated
80g plain flour
1 egg, beaten
2 slices white bread, made into breadcrumbs
4 tbsp olive oil
20g butter

Preheat the oven to 180°C/350°F/Gas 4.

To make the potato cakes, cook the cavolo nero in a small saucepan with some water, stirring often until wilted. Drain well and chop the leaves finely. Place the mashed potato, mascarpone, Parmesan and cavolo nero in a bowl and mix together. Season well. Divide the mixture into four balls, shape them into cakes and place in the fridge to firm up until ready to cook.

Meanwhile, place the John Dory fillets in a flat oven dish and brush with the melted butter. Season and keep chilled until ready to cook.

Coat the potato cakes with flour, dusting off any excess, then dip into the egg, coating evenly. Finally coat well with breadcrumbs. Heat the oil and butter in a frying pan, add the potato cakes, and cook on a medium heat for about 4 minutes each side. Now finish off in the oven for another 12 minutes.

To cook the fish, place the tray with the fillets in the hot oven for about 8–10 minutes until they are just cooked and flake easily.

To serve, place a potato cake in the centre of each plate and top with a John Dory fillet. Garnish with basil leaves and drizzle over with some oil.

COST £ 11.50

SUMMER TIRAMISÙ

August is the month to enjoy blueberries. The European variety is always smaller in size than the American imports, but size is not an indication of flavour and taste. Mix with other berries and enjoy this variation to the classic recipe for tiramisù! This recipe will serve about ten, so there will be plenty for the day after, when the tiramisù is even better.

1 Madeira sponge, about 20cm long and cut in 2cm thick slices
200ml strong coffee
5 tbsp Amaretto (an almond liqueur)
5 eggs, separated
150g caster sugar
250g mascarpone cheese
500ml double cream
300g blueberries or mixed berries
cocoa powder to dust

Arrange the sponge slices to cover the base of a suitably large dish. Brush liberally with the coffee and the Amaretto.

Whip the egg yolks with two-thirds of the sugar until pale and creamy. In a separate bowl, whisk the mascarpone and then mix in with the egg yolk mixture. Whip the cream and add to the egg yolk mix. Finally whisk the egg whites separately with the remaining sugar until glossy and stiff. Fold the egg whites into the egg yolk and mascarpone mixture.

Spread some of the cream mixture on the sponge base and top with some berries. Repeat these layers with the remaining ingredients, finishing with the mascarpone cream as the top layer.

Leave in the fridge overnight. Dust with cocoa just before serving.

COST £6.10

THE WINE SELECTION

For this utterly scrumptious menu I have invented a summer
cocktail to celebrate its toothsomeness. I have yet to give it a name
(and welcome suggestions) but it is supremely simple and the
perfect accompaniment to cooking, doing the crossword, reading, or
listening to music. First, we pour a slug of **Rocks Organic Orange
Concentrate (20 points, £1.99, Sainsbury's)** into a large stemmed
glass and on to it I have sloshed the remains of a four-day-old
opened bottle of champagne, still sparkling (thanks to my fridge and
an airtight clip-on-clip-off seal). A cheap cava would do instead, of
course; the end result is fantastic either way. The acidity of the
bubbles and the richness and tanginess of the orange are just magic
together.

As is, to get down to the job in hand, **Sainsbury's** non-vintage
Sicilian White (15.5 points, £2.99) with that tricky first course (the
tomatoes are rich enough, Silvena, without the cinnamon and the
sultanas). This tremendous bargain of a bottle has a pleasant double
layer of soft under-ripe peach and then lemon zest and will charm
those toms into polite submission. May I suggest three bottles? For
this wine will also, elegantly, take care of those fillets of John Dory
with their extravagant mascarpone potato cake. This wine has several
winning virtues but one of its strongest is its screwcap, so it will stay
fresh and frisky for almost as long as you will (well, not quite
perhaps, but you get my point).

We have, then, blown £8.97 on the wine which leaves us with just
£1.03 for something to go with that tiramisù with its blueberries.
This seeming impossibility is solved by circularity; ie you serve the
cocktail I mentioned above. I offer this idea for free, so you can put
the £1.03 towards the cost of the fish fillets.

On the other hand it does seem a little mean to that wonderful pud
to palm it off with an aperitif. So let's be a little extravagant and grab
a bottle of **Sainsbury's Rich Cream Sherry**. Prosaic by name,
ambrosiac by nature, but it just happens to be one of the richest
dessert wine bargains around. I happen to believe that if it didn't say
sherry, didn't claim to be cream rich, and didn't have the name of a
great big supermarket in front of it, and was given a jazzier name
and a sexier label, it would sell like, well, hot cakes (with which, of
course, it is splendidly capable of going). It's composed of crème
brûlée and honey yet it is neither too sweet nor too cloying. It can
be poured over ice-cream to great effect. It rates **16.5 points**, costs
£3.99 and really is a bargain sweet wine of great charm and
concentration.

BULGARIAN MEATBALL SOUP

I claim this as Bulgarian, but the cuisine of neighbouring Turkey has had a considerable influence on this soup as it has had on many other Bulgarian dishes. The soup also has strong Jewish influences, as there is a rather large Jewish community in Bulgaria. This soup is the favourite of any child back home, as it is a whole meal in one pot. The meatballs are cooked in the soup broth instead of being browned separately as is usually done with meatballs.

1 litre chicken stock (see page 197)
2 large potatoes, peeled and grated
1 large carrot, peeled and grated
2 tbsp plain yoghurt
1 egg yolk
2 tbsp lemon juice
3 tbsp finely chopped parsley

Meatballs
200g veal mince
200g pork mince
1 large slice crusty bread, crust removed, soaked in water and
    squeezed dry
½ onion, finely chopped
salt and pepper
1 tbsp plain flour

For the meatballs, combine the veal and pork mince, bread and onion in a large bowl. Season to taste and mix well until all holds together. Shape the mixture into small meatballs, about 2cm in diameter. Roll in the plain flour and shake off the excess.

Bring the chicken stock to the boil in a large saucepan. Drop the meatballs in and add the grated potato and carrot. Simmer for about 20 minutes until the meatballs are cooked.

Meanwhile in a small bowl mix the yoghurt, egg yolk and lemon juice. Add some of the soup liquid to this, then return the mixture to the pot of soup. Mix well and heat through briefly.

Sprinkle the soup with parsley and serve hot.

COST £5.80

BULGARIAN AUBERGINE MOUSSAKA

There are many recipes for aubergine moussaka: some have extra vegetables, like courgettes and potatoes; others have a topping of cheese béchamel sauce. The one thing to remember when cooking aubergine is that when fried, it absorbs massive amounts of oil, so therefore you must work quickly. At the same time you must make sure that the aubergine is cooked fully, as it will taste bitter if under-cooked.

    2 large aubergines
    olive oil
    salt and pepper
    1 large onion, finely chopped
    4 garlic cloves, crushed
    400g lamb mince
    1 x 400 can plum tomatoes
    1 tbsp finely chopped oregano
    2 tbsp finely chopped parsley
    2 large beef tomatoes

Peel the aubergines and slice them lengthwise into 5mm thick long oval slices.

In a large and heavy non-stick pan, heat some olive oil and sauté the aubergine slices, a few at a time, turning them over and making sure that they are evenly browned and cooked. Using a slotted spatula, transfer to kitchen paper to drain off the excess fat. Sprinkle with salt. Repeat this until you have cooked all the aubergine slices, adding more oil when needed. Keep the aubergine slices in a cool place until ready to use.

Preheat the oven to 180°C/350°F/Gas 4, and have ready a medium 15 x 10 x 4cm baking dish, lightly greased with oil.

Now prepare the moussaka filling. In a large and heavy saucepan, warm 2 tbsp oil and sauté the onion and garlic for about 5 minutes. Add the lamb mince and cook until the meat is browned. Add the canned tomatoes and their juices, and simmer for a further 10 minutes. Season to taste and add the oregano and parsley.

Slice the large beef tomatoes horizontally into 5mm slices and keep aside until ready to use.

To assemble the moussaka, line the bottom of the dish with a third of the aubergine slices, slightly overlapping, and top with half of the lamb mixture, then cover again with half of the remaining aubergine slices and the second half of the meat mixture. Cover with the remaining aubergine slices and finish with the tomato slices, arranging them on the top of the moussaka. Cover the dish tightly with foil and place in a large oven tray half filled with hot water. Bake in the preheated oven for 40 minutes.

Remove the foil and the baking dish from the water bath and return the moussaka to the oven for a further 10 minutes to brown. Serve warm.

COST £6.80

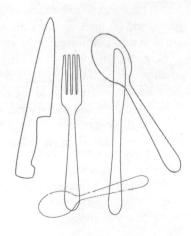

POACHED PEARS with WHITE CHOCOLATE SABAYON

This elegant and richly satisfying dessert is great for those who want a little chocolate at the end of a meal without being completely subjected to 'death by chocolate'! The pears are simply poached in a mixture of sweet wine and sugar syrup and then served with a drizzle of a light white chocolate sabayon.

    4 Williams pears, peeled, halved and cored
    2 cinnamon sticks
    100ml Sauternes wine
    100ml sugar syrup (see page 200)
    1 vanilla pod, split
    3 tbsp lemon juice
    White chocolate sabayon
    4 egg yolks
    2 tbsp sugar syrup (see page 200)
    30g white chocolate, finely chopped
    50ml double cream

Combine the pears, cinnamon, Sauternes, sugar syrup, vanilla and lemon juice in a saucepan and bring to the boil. Cover with parchment paper, and simmer for 20 minutes until the pear halves are tender. Leave to cool in the syrup.

Make the sabayon by whisking the egg yolks and sugar syrup in a small pan or bowl that is sitting over a pan of simmering water. Whisk for at least 10 minutes. Add the chocolate and mix well to melt. Allow to cool and then fold in the double cream.

Serve the pears with a spoonful of their own juices and drizzle. around them the white chocolate sabayon.

COST £7.10

THE WINE SELECTION

Bulgarian meatball soup? Oh please, Silvena! This is what they serve criminals in Sofia prison, isn't it? And then I taste the dish and...oooh...yes! Any vacancies in Sofia prison? There must exist an irresistible conviction to commit crime in Bulgaria if lags are dished out this soup (which has a wonderful, life-enhancing, mother-earthiness). If the stock is as pertinent as it should be, home-made and slightly oleaginous, then this is a stunning way to begin a meal (a meal in itself, really). Of course I can take the easy way out here and suggest various Bulgarian wines to go with the soup, and with the moussaka to follow, and if you turn to the second menu in spring you will find several excellent candidate reds to handle both courses. But cannot we be a bit more imaginative here? With one leap it is easy to imagine that soup cooked by my paternal grandmother; and her chicken soup, which I consumed but once, changed my life (I was five at the time) for it forever changed my view of soups. Silvena's soup is in the same league: not a thin stringy liquid with a few dead veggies floating in it, but a vibrant dish upon which heroes can feed. Thus a heroic wine, like a pungent Pinot Noir (not unlike

the cheapie discussed in menu 8 in spring, but richer and gamier), is to be found for that soup and it must be one which can also carry on with that moussaka. Shall we, then, try **Mount Difficulty Pinot Noir 2001** (**16 points**, **£16.99**, **Sainsbury's**)? This splendid New Zealand Pinot improves in bottle every time I taste it and it is one of the few Kiwi Pinots to have disciplined tannins and a lovely gamey dryness. Other excellent Pinot Noirs, also from New Zealand, are **Wither Hills**, **Jackson Estate** and **Villa Maria** (the **Cellar Selection 2002**, **16 points**, around a **tenner** is especially tasty). But all these Pinots serve our purpose, especially in the 2002 vintage (because I went out there and personally caressed the grapes, that's why, and it seems to have made all the difference). Too pricey? Then try **Prahova Valley Pinot Noir Reserve 2000** (**16 points**, **£3.98**, **Asda**) from Romania.

Wine wise, however, this meal has not yet reached its high point. That is reserved for the pears with their hideously scrumptious white chocolate poured over. It seems to me we might just drink the Sauternes you used in preparing the dish. **Waitrose** has **Château Bastor-Lamontagne Sauternes 1999** (**15 points** now, 18 points in six to eight years, **£25.00**). It has intense honied richness with nuts, orange blossom and ripe melon (sweet). A pear-and-sabayon wine now or cellar it to achieve greater richness and aroma. Same goes for **Château Liot Sauternes 2001** (**15 points** now, 18.5 points in ten years' time, **£9.79** the half bottle). It has loose-knit honey, pineapple, toffee and cream which will coalesce more excitingly in time. One way to achieve greater perfection with a wine yet to reach its peak is to decant it and so I suggest you transfer the whole contents of either of these Sauternes into a water jug and place it in the door of the refrigerator. You can do this at breakfast, for they will both excitingly, sensuously expand with twelve hours of total breathing and still be drinkable two days later.

KIOPOLU (BULGARIAN AUBERGINE SALAD)

When I used to cook at Books for Cooks, I often did this salad, and without fail, everyone was most impressed every time, and used to ask for the recipe. In the Mediterranean it is known as aubergine caviar, and sometimes yoghurt, tahini or mayonnaise are added. The secret of the success of this salad is the smoky flavour of the cooked aubergines. Serve with flatbread.

    2 large aubergines
    juice of 2 lemons
    4 tbsp olive oil
    4 garlic cloves, crushed
    salt and pepper
    5 tbsp chopped parsley
    50g shelled walnuts, coarsely chopped

Place the aubergines straight on the gas ring on the naked flame and cook like that, turning over with a long-handled fork, until the whole aubergine is charred and soft. If you have an electric cooker, then you can place the whole aubergine on top of your hot plate and cook as above.

Place the cooked aubergines in a colander and cool. When cool enough to handle, peel off the blackened skin and discard. Squeeze the aubergines dry. Chop the flesh and place in a large bowl.

Add the lemon juice, olive oil, garlic and salt and pepper to taste, mix well and adjust the seasoning. Sprinkle with the parsley and chopped walnuts. Serve cold with pitta or any other flatbread.

COST £2.50

LOBSTER in GALANGAL, LEMONGRASS and SPRING ONION BROTH

To cook the lobsters from raw, put in the freezer two hours before cooking, which will kill them painlessly. Have a large pan with boiling salted water ready and add the lobsters. Bring to the boil again and cook for about 4 minutes. This way the lobsters will still be partly raw and will enable you to finish cooking by using the different method below.

> 2 live lobsters, about 450g each, killed as above
> vegetable oil for deep-frying
> 1 tsp salt
> ½ tsp caster sugar
> 1 tbsp dark soy sauce
> 1 tbsp oyster sauce
> 1 tsp sesame oil
> 2 tbsp Chinese rice wine
> 2 tbsp cornflour
> 2 tbsp crushed garlic
> 2 lemongrass sticks, peeled and soft white parts finely chopped
> 120g fresh galangal, peeled and thinly sliced
> 2 bunches spring onions, thinly sliced
> 250ml chicken stock (see page 197)

Cut the boiled lobsters in half lengthwise from the head down to the tail. Separate the head from the tail and cut each tail half into three pieces. Remove the stomach sac. Chop off the claws and crack the shells. Discard the legs.

Heat the oil for deep-frying to 190°C/375°F. Mix the salt, sugar, soy sauce, oyster sauce, sesame oil and Chinese rice wine in a bowl and set aside.

Sprinkle the lobster bits with the cornflour and deep-fry in two to three batches for 2–3 minutes. Drain on absorbent kitchen paper.

Heat 3 tbsp oil in a wok. Add the garlic, lemongrass, galangal and spring onions and stir-fry for a few minutes. Add the lobster to the wok with the soy sauce mixture and stir-fry for 2 more minutes. Add the chicken stock and simmer for 3–4 more minutes. Serve some lobster with some broth in deep serving plates.

COST £14.50

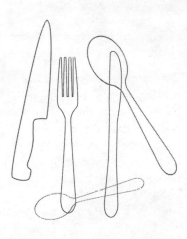

WHITE CHOCOLATE PANNACOTTA

This recipe is perfect for both chocolate and pannacotta lovers! It is rich and smooth in texture, but still very creamy. You can serve it with milk chocolate shavings and have a delicious chocolate dessert, or you can serve it with seasonal berries instead to offset the strong flavours.

> 500ml double cream
> 100g caster sugar
> 100g white chocolate, finely chopped
> 3 gelatine leaves

Place the cream, sugar and chocolate in a small saucepan and slowly simmer until the sugar and chocolate have melted.

Place the gelatine in a bowl of cold water to soften. When soft, squeeze dry, add to the cream mixture and heat until the gelatine has dissolved.

Pour the mixture into four small moulds and refrigerate overnight.

Cost £2.80

THE WINE SELECTION

Goodness, did the dear lady keep this to last as a deliberate ploy? Bulgarian aubergine salad, my life! Ah, what memories! Oh yes, when I first met Silvena at Books for Cooks she gave me this dish and I exulted to eat it. What wine I brought with me I can't remember (I used to go to the shop regularly as it was in the street I once lived in in Notting Hill and I often arrived with six bottles I'd previously opened for tasting purposes). The secret of the dish, Silvena advises us, is the smoky flavour of the cooked aubergines and this is the secret of finding the wine to drink with them. We need a rich white wine, one which will also take us, effortlessly, on to, into, and past, that exotic lobster dish. There is one region in the world to which we can turn for help. It is Alsace and the wine is **Réserve du Baron de Turckheim Alsace Gewürztraminer 2000 (17 points, £6.01, Asda)**. Now this wine's in fact from a single vineyard, Herrenweg. And it is a lovely wine. It has very dry spicy rose-petal fruit – hint of apricot here as well – and the class is outstanding for the money. It will, I feel, gain by cellaring for two to four years when it will get oilier and more sensual. This wine is happy to mix it with the aubergines and lobster, even one with galangal, lemongrass and spring onion broth (and we can afford two lobsters on our budget? Oh, well, let it pass).

With the white chocolate pannacotta, since I have been so parsimonious with the wine (speaking comparatively with my chef's idea of an economy menu), I am going to go for **Villard Estate Casablanca Botrytis Sauvignon Blanc 2000** from Chile. It has a burned undertone, entirely congenial, and it leaves the palate with an undertone of nuts and raspberry crème brûlée. The frontal attack is spicy pineapple with soft, bruised pear with firm acids. It rates **17 points** and costs **£8.99** the half bottle at **D. Byrne, Great Northern Wine Company** and **Wiland Wines**. It is a fabulous pudding wine, fit for any pud by any chef in any situation in the world. And fit to end any meal in the world (and to end this book).

BASIC RECIPES

CHICKEN STOCK

Makes about 1.5 litres

1 large onion
3 celery sticks
2 leeks
20g butter
1 bay leaf
1 garlic clove, halved
a few sprigs parsley
3 black peppercorns
1.5kg raw chicken carcasses, chopped
2.5 litres water

Cut all the vegetables into small dice. In a large saucepan melt the butter and sauté the vegetables briefly without colouring.

Add the bay leaf, garlic, parsley, peppercorns and chicken bones. Cover with the cold water and simmer, skimming frequently, for about 2 hours. Strain.

The stock is now ready to use. You can freeze it as well as keep it chilled in the fridge (for two days).

VEGETABLE STOCK

Makes about 1 litre

200g carrots
4 celery sticks
1 leek
1 fennel bulb
3 tbsp vegetable oil
1 bay leaf
a handful each of thyme and parsley
5 white peppercorns
1 tsp coriander seeds
1/2 lemon, sliced
1.5 litres water

Cut all the vegetables into small dice. Heat the oil in a large heavy saucepan and sauté the chopped vegetables, without browning.

Add the herbs, peppercorns, coriander, lemon and water. Simmer for 30 minutes until the liquid has reduced.

The stock is now ready and you can strain out the vegetables through a sieve. You should have about 1.1 litres stock: if you have more than this, than bring the stock back to the boil and reduce further. The more you reduce the stock, the more intense the flavour will be. Store in the fridge for up to two days, or freeze.

FISH STOCK

Makes about 1.5 litres

1 large onion
1 leek
1 small fennel bulb
2 celery sticks
50g butter
a handful of parsley
1 bay leaf
6 white peppercorns
800g white fish (sole or turbot) bones, chopped
200ml white wine
2 litres water

Slice the onion, and chop the leek, fennel and celery into small pieces. In a heavy large saucepan, sweat the vegetables in the butter without colouring. Add the parsley, bay leaf and peppercorns.

Place the fish bones on top of the vegetables, cover with the wine and cook until almost dry.

Now add the water and simmer for no more than 20 minutes. Sieve through a sieve and keep the stock in the fridge until ready to use (no more than two days). You can freeze the stock as well.

LAMB STOCK

2kg raw lamb bones
2 large Spanish onions, chopped
2 large carrots, chopped
3 celery sticks, chopped
3 garlic cloves
2 tbsp vegetable oil
2 tomatoes, chopped
150ml red wine
1 bay leaf
10 black peppercorns
2 litres cold water

Preheat the oven to 200°C/400°F/Gas 6, and roast the bones for an hour or until golden brown, turning every now and again to brown evenly.

In a large saucepan, sauté the onion, carrot, celery and garlic in the oil until slightly browned, about 8 minutes. Add the tomato and cook for a further 2 minutes. Add the wine and cook until it has almost all evaporated.

Add the browned bones, bay leaf and peppercorns, and the cold water to cover. Bring to the boil and then simmer uncovered for at least 3–4 hours, until the liquid is reduced to less than half. You will need to skim every now and again.

Strain and reserve in the fridge until ready to use, for about two days. You can freeze the stock at this stage in small containers, and use as and when needed.

PESTO

Makes about 200g

> 50g pine nuts, toasted
> 3 garlic cloves, crushed
> 2 bunches basil
> 60g Parmesan, freshly grated
> 180ml olive oil
> salt and pepper

Place the pine nuts, garlic, basil and Parmesan in a food processor and blend. At the same time pour the olive oil into the processor in a thin stream to create a thick paste. Season to taste.

The pesto is now ready and can be stored in the fridge for at least four to five days.

SUGAR SYRUP

Makes about 600ml

> 500ml water
> 440g caster sugar

Bring the water and sugar to the boil. Simmer for just a few minutes until the sugar is completely dissolved. Remove from the heat and cool.

The syrup is now ready to use and can be stored in the fridge for up to a month.

Variation
For vanilla syrup, add a split vanilla pod and proceed as above.

CRÈME PÂTISSIÈRE OR PASTRY CREAM   Makes about 500g

6 egg yolks
125g caster sugar
40g plain flour
500ml milk
1/2 tsp vanilla extract

Whisk the egg yolks with half of the sugar until creamy and pale in colour. Sift in the flour and mix gently.

Bring the milk and the remaining sugar to the boil, and slowly pour into the egg mixture, stirring continuously. Pour this cream back into the saucepan, add the vanilla extract, and cook over a very gentle heat until it is thickened, about 2 minutes, stirring all the time.

Have ready a large container filled with cold water and ice, and drop the saucepan in it as soon as it is off the heat, so you stop the cooking process. The crème pâtissière is now ready.

WINE SUPPLIERS

ADNAMS WINE MERCHANTS

Sole Bay Brewery, East Green,
Southwold, Suffolk IP18 6JW
Tel: (01502) 727222
Fax: (01502) 727223
E-mail: wines@adnams.co.uk
Website: www.adnamswines.co.uk

ALDI

Holly Lane,
Atherstone, Warwickshire CV9 2SQ
Tel: (01827) 711800
Fax: (01827) 710899
Customer help-line: (0805) 134262
Website: www.aldi.com

ASDA

Head Office, Asda House,
Southbank, Great Wilson Street,
Leeds LS11 5AD
Tel: (0500) 100055 (230 branches nationwide)
Fax: (0113) 2417732
Website: www.asda.co.uk

BOOTHS

Head Office, Booths Distribution Centre,
Bluebell Way
Ribbleton, Preston PR2 5PY
Tel: (freephone) 0800 072011
     (01772) 483540
Fax: (01772) 483541

BUDGENS

Stonefield Way,
Ruislip, Middlesex HA4 0JR
Tel: (020) 8422 9511
Customer Services:
Tel: (0800) 526 002
Fax: (020) 8864 2800
E-mail: info@budgens.co.uk
Website: www.budgens.com

ANTHONY BYRNE FINE WINES

Ramsey Business Park, Ramsey,
Huntingdon, Cambridgeshire PE26 2UR
Tel: (01487) 814555
Fax: (01487) 814962
E-mail: info@abfw.co.uk
Website: www.abfw.co.uk

D. BYRNE & CO.

Victoria Building, 12 King Street,
Clitheroe, Yorkshire BB7 2EP
Tel: (01200) 423152

CO-OP

PO Box 53, New Century House,
Manchester M60 4ES
Tel: (0161) 834 1212
Website: www.co-op.co.uk

RODNEY DENSEM WINES LTD

Regent House, Lancaster Fields,
Crewe Gates Farm Estate,
Crewe, Cheshire CW1 6FF
Tel: (01270) 212200
Fax: (01270) 212300
E-mail: info@buywineonline.co.uk
Website: www.buywineonline.co.uk

EVERYWINE
Tel: (01772) 329700
Fax: (01772) 329709
E-mail: admin@everywine.co.uk
Website: www.everywine.co.uk

FINE & RARE WINES LTD
Pall Mall Deposit,
124–128 Barlby Road, London W10 6BL
Tel: (020) 8960 1995
Fax: (020) 8960 1911
E-mail: wine@frw.co.uk
Website: www.frw.co.uk

GREAT NORTHERN WINE COMPANY
The Warehouse, Blossomgate,
Ripon, North Yorkshire HG4 ??AJ
Tel: (01765) 606767
Fax: (01765) 609151
E-mail: info@greatnorthernwine.com
Website: www.greatnorthernwine.com

HARRODS
Brompton Road, Knightsbridge,
London SW1X 7XL
Tel: (020) 7730 1234
Fax: (020) 7581 0470
E-mail: food.halls@harrods.com
Website: www.harrods.com

HAYNES, HANSON AND CLARK
25 Eccleston Street,
London SW1W 9NP
Tel: (020) 7259 0102
Fax: (020) 7259 0103
E-mail: london@hhandc.co.uk

CHARLES HENNINGS (VINTNERS) LTD

The Wine Cellars, Station Approach
Pulborough, West Sussex RH20 1AQ
Tel: (01798) 872485
Fax: (01798) 873163
E-mail: sales@chv-wine.co.uk
Website: www.chv-wine.co.uk

IPSWICH WINES AND BEERS WHOLESALE LTD

Units 12 & 16 Foxtail Road, Ransomes Euro Park,
Ipswich, Suffolk IP3 9RT
Tel: (01473) 715125

S.H. JONES & CO.

The Old Wine House, 27 High Street,
Banbury, Oxfordshire OX16 5EW
Tel: (01295) 251179

RICHARD KIHL

Slaughden Wines, 140–142 High Street,
Aldeburgh, Suffolk IP15 5AQ
Tel: (01728) 454455
Fax: (010728) 454433
E-mail: sales@richardkihl.ltd.uk
Website: www.richardkihl.ltd.uk

MAJESTIC

Head Office, Majestic House,
Otterspool Way, Watford,
Hertfordshire WD25 8WW
Tel: (01923) 298200
Fax: (01923) 819105
E-mail: info@majestic.co.uk
Website: www.majestic.co.uk

MARKS & SPENCER

Waterside House,
35 North Wharf Road,
London w2 1nw
Customer services:
Tel: (0845) 302 1234
E-mail: customer.services@marks-and-spencer.com
Website: www.marksandspencer.com

MORRISON'S

Hillmore House, Thornton Road,
Bradford, Yorkshire bd8 9ax
Tel: (01274) 494166
Fax: (01274) 494831
Website: www.morereasons.co.uk

NOBLE ROT WINE WAREHOUSES LTD

18 Market Street, Bromsgrove,
Worcestershire b61 8da
Tel: (01527) 575606
Fax: (01527) 833133
E-mail: info@nrwinewarehouse.co.uk
Website: www.nrwinewarehouse.co.uk

ODDBINS

31–33 Weir Road,
Wimbledon, London sw19 8ug
Tel: (020) 8944 4400
Fax: (020) 8944 4411
E-mail: customer.service@oddbinsmail.com
Website: www.oddbins.com

PECKHAM & RYE

21 Clarence Drive,
Glasgow, Lanarkshire g12 9qn
Tel: (0141) 3344312

THOS PEATLING FINE WINES

Westgate House, Bury St Edmunds,
Suffolk IP33 1QS
Tel: (01284) 755948
Fax: (01284) 714483
E-mail: sales@thospeatling.co.uk
Website: www.thospeatling.co.uk

PENISTONE COURT WINE CELLARS

Railway Station, Penistone,
Sheffield, South Yorkshire S36 6H9
Tel: (01226) 766037

CHRISTOPHER PIPER WINES

1 Silver Street, Ottery St Mary,
Devon EX11 1DB
Tel: (01404) 814139
Fax: (01404) 812100
Website: www.christopherpiperwines.co.uk

PORTLAND WINE COMPANY

16 North Parade, Sale,
Cheshire M33 3JS
Tel: (0161) 9628752
Fax: (0161) 9051291
E-mail: portwineco@aol.com
Website: www.portlandwine.co.uk

ROBERTS & SPEIGHT

40 Norwood, Beverley,
East Yorkshire HU17 9EY
Tel: (01482) 870717
Fax: (01482) 870717
E-mail: sales@robertsandspeight.co.uk
Website: www.robertsandspeight.co.uk

SAFEWAY

Safeway House, 6 Millington Road,
Hayes, Middlesex UB3 4AY
Tel: (020) 8848 8744
Fax: (020) 8573 1865
E-mail: safewaypressoffice@btclick.com
Website: www.safeway.co.uk

SAINSBURY'S

Head Office, 33 High Holborn,
London ECIN 2HT
Tel: (020) 7695 6000
Fax: (020) 7695 7610
Customer Careline: (0800) 636262
Website: www.sainsburys.co.uk

SANDHAMS WINE MERCHANTS

3 South Street, Caistor,
Lincolnshire LN7 6UB
Tel: (01472) 852118
Fax: (01472) 852118
E-mail: enquiries@shopping4wine.co.uk
Website: www.sandhamswines.co.uk

SOHO WINE SUPPLY

18 Percy Street,
London WIT 1DX
Tel: (020) 7636 8490
Fax: (020) 7636 8899
E-mail: info@sohowine.co.uk
Website: www.sohowine.co.uk

SOMERFIELD

Somerfield House, Whitchurch Lane,
Bristol BS14 OTJ
Tel: (0117) 935 9359
Fax: (0117) 978 0629
E-mail: customer.service@somerfield.co.uk
Website: www.somerfield.co.uk

TESCO

Head Office, Tesco House,
PO Box 18, Delamare Road,
Cheshunt, Hertfordshire EN8 9SL
Tel: (01992) 632222
Customer Services helpline: (0800) 505555
E-mail: customer.service@tesco.co.uk
Website: www.tesco.com

THRESHER

Enjoyment Hall, Bessemer Road,
Welwyn Garden City, Hertfordshire AL7 1BL
Tel: (01707) 387200
Fax: (01707) 387416
Website: www.enjoyment.co.uk

UNWINS

Birchwood House, Victoria Road,
Dartford, Kent DA1 5AJ
Tel: (01322) 272711
Fax: (01322) 294469
E-mail: admin@unwinswines.co.uk
Website: www.unwins.co.uk

VALVONA & CROLLA LTD

19 Elm Row,
Edinburgh EH7 4AA
Tel: (0131) 556 6066
Fax: (0131) 556 1668
E-mail: wine@valvonacrolla.co.uk
Website: www.valvonacrolla.co.uk

J. WADSWORTH

34 The Broadway, St Ives,
Cambridgeshire PE27 5BN
Tel: (01480) 463522
E-mail: enquiries@wadsworthwines.co.uk
Website: www.wadsworthwines.co.uk

WAITROSE

Head Office, Doncaster Road,
Southern Industrial Area,
Bracknell, Berkshire RH12 8YA
Tel: (01344) 424 680

Waitrose Wine Direct
Tel: (0800) 188881
Fax: (0800) 188888
E-mail: customerservice@waitrose.co.uk
Website: www.waitrose.com

WILAND WINES

83 Hollow Road, Anstey,
Leicester, Leicestershire LE7 7FR
Tel: (0116) 2364251

WINE SOCIETY

Members' Shop and HQ,
Gunnels Wood Road, Stevenage,
Hertfordshire SG1 2BG
Tel: (01438) 741177
Fax: (01438) 741392
E-mail: memberservice@thewinesociety.com
Website: www.thewinesociety.com

RECIPE INDEX

WINE INDEX

ACKNOWLEDGEMENTS

Silvena and I would first like to thank Ian Katz, editor of the *Guardian*'s G2 supplement in which, on alternate Wednesdays, the 'Party Paupers' column, on which this book is based, first appeared. Our thanks are also due to the *Guardian*'s Pascal Wyse, Merope Mills and Leslie Plommer. Sarah Gilbert, on the picture desk, is thanked for her efforts. We would also to express our gratitude to our commissioning editor Denise Bates, our editor Susan Fleming, our agent Felicity Rubinstein, and our designer Bob Vickers, who has turned what looked like a dog's dinner into a very elegant book indeed.

MALCOLM GLUCK is wine correspondent of the *Guardian* newspaper. He has been writing the Superplonk column for 15 years. He has written some two dozen books on wine, including *The Sensational Liquid*, a wine-tasting manual, and *Wine Matters – Why Water Just Won't Do*. He presented BBC-2's TV series, 'Gluck Gluck Gluck', and has compiled a wine-related classical music cd set for Deutsche Grammophon. He is presently working on four further books for 2005 on wine/food/travel/photography.

SILVENA ROWE, a Bulgarian, has lived in London for the last 18 years, having worked as a chef, chef-presenter, food writer and culinary consultant. Her cooking career started at a very early age as a 'greedy child' in a home where all was centred on good home-made, wholesome food.

As a recognised cookery demonstrator, Silvena has been associated with Books for Cooks, Mosimann's Academy and Baker and Spice, as well as presenting on major national food shows. She has appeared on Channel 4's 'Chef on the Night'. Currently Silvena has a regular cookery column in the *Guardian* and also freelances as a food writer for magazines and newspapers. In addition, Silvena is also involved in consultancy work and product development with major UK food retailers and menu consultancy for leading restaurants.

Silvena is married with two sons and lives in London.

Has **SUPERGRUB** made you hungry for more?

Then dip into **SUPERPLONK 2005**

Malcolm Gluck's unique guide to the top 1,000 wines in supermarkets and high-street stores. No other wine writer rates wines on a value-for-money basis.